MW01089143

DIVINE SELF-INVESTMENT

AN OPEN AND RELATIONAL
CONSTRUCTIVE CHRISTOLOGY

TRIPP FULLER

STUDIES IN OPEN AND RELATIONAL THEOLOGIES

 **Sacra**Sage

SacraSagePress.com

© 2020 SacraSage Press and Tripp Fuller

Print: 978-1-948609-29-6
Electronic: 978-1-948609-30-2
Printed in the United States of America

Library of Congress Cataloguing-in-Publication Data
Divine Self-Investment: An Open and Relational Constructive Theology / Tripp Fuller

Studies in Open and Relational Theologies *promotes academic research and discourse on open, relational, and process perspectives in theology and religion (including those of open theism, process theology, neoclassical, and other relational and personalist traditions). This series is devoted to constructive and critical studies, especially those involving theological and philosophical speculation about the nature of Ultimates, freedom, power, relationality, evil, love, religious belonging, and more.*

For Elgin & Elgin

ABSTRACT

In this project, I investigate the possibility of a robust constructive open and relational Christology. To do this, I lay out a broadly open and relational vision, situate the constructive function of contemporary historical Jesus research, and propose three pairings of contemporary Christologies that share a thematic center with distinct trajectories. I intend to both articulate each thinkers' own contribution and stretch them toward each other. The goal is to move toward a three-pronged constructive Christology that engages historical Jesus studies and seeks to speak in both an existential and metaphysical register. In sum, it will be argued that the Christologically tinged existential starting point for Christology requires all three, and that more potential for robust account is present in the examined theologians than often assumed. To conclude, I will return to an open and relational account of God, allowing the Christological investigations to thematize its commitments, and propose a centering metaphor for an open and relational vision—namely the self-investment of God.

Table of Contents

The Logos Liberally Applied
Staging the Incarnation
Divine Initiative and Promise
The Word of Creation and Word for Salvation

A Liberal Protestant's Christology of the Heart
The Creator is the Redeemer
The Revelatory Nature of the Christ Event
The Transferable Nightmare of the Cross
From the Heart of the Disciple to the Heart of God
The Gospels and Han
The Cross in the Heart of God
Identification and Solidarity in the Process of Salvation

"You are the Christ, Son of the Living God"
Contingency and Christology
"The Spirit of the Lord is Upon Me"
"The Fruit of the Vine of David"
"Image of the Invisible God"
Re-Staging the Incarnation in the History of God
"Get Behind Me Satan"
Divine Self-Investment Beyond the Cross

1

INTRODUCTION

Theological Significance

Christian theology has always been about God, but the God of whom Christians speak has always been tied to Jesus of Nazareth. Historically, the church emerged out of Second Temple Period Judaism and the texts, tradition, and history of Israel are essential for understanding Christianity; and yet the earliest confession that "Jesus is Lord" marked a significant distinction within the community. For Christians, the answer to the question "Who is God?" required telling the story of Jesus. What Jesus said, did, endured, and delivered definitively shape the Christian life and the community's understanding of God. While the concept of God was shaped by Jesus from the beginning, the explanation and justification for it has a history. We are at a moment in this history in which the Christian community is struggling anew to articulate the ongoing encounter with the God that Jesus mediates.

While our present situation may bring the Christological endeavor a host of fresh challenges, it is not unique to our history that the central confession of the faith is problematic. To identify a crucified Rabbi from the past as the image of the invisible God, the first-born of all creation, and the second person of the Trinity, are and always has been a deeply contested affirmation. It is also a deeply personal affirmation. In one sense, it is personal in that the individual disciple in each ecclesiastical expression responds to the call Christ gave to his disciples, but it is also personal in that the heart of any Christian response to God is an affirmation of God's presence in the person of Jesus. Today, however, the question of Jesus' person is not the only contested identity. Unlike most of the church's history, our cultural situation problematizes not just the conclusion of believers, but the believers themselves. Any attempt to understand the contemporary Christology requires that one deal with both sides of this personal problem.

For the Christian theologian, the Christological predicament has a number of important features that need to be acknowledged and addressed to pursue a tradition, the Jesus of history, the Trinitarian event that gives the context for hearing and speaking the gospel, or a foundation established from an inquiry external to the tradition itself, such as the phenomena of religion. In much the same way, the concept of God was continually problematized and marginalized. God was increasingly unnecessary for the dominant accounts of our cosmos or human distinctiveness, as a justification for our morality or Western civilization, and the concept of God was dispersed from the center of town to the private study of some but not all people. God was no longer simply assumed, and was no longer necessary for the engaged citizen. It is hard to overstate how significant the cultural shift was for constructive theologians. The reality of God could not be assumed nor persuasively demonstrated. The historical Jesus called into question the theo-logic formed in Greek, thrust his Jewishness before our eyes, and made Lessing's ditch a permanent feature for the contemporary disciple.

The goal for this project is to take the problems facing constructive Christology seriously and insist that Christology, or at least the confessional identification of Jesus as the Christ, inherently problematizes the dominant solutions to our predicament. Should an adequate constructive Christology be possible for our contemporary situation, it must address three distinct hesitations that shape most proposals.

The Historical Conundrum

First, it must acknowledge and address both the content and more importantly open-ended nature of the quest for the historical Jesus. Christology requires that there was a historical Jesus. However, just because the reality of the historical referent can be established does not satisfy the demand. The ongoing and ever-open nature of the quest means that the historical datum and their ensuing constructions will not cease. While the content of the quest can and should affect our Christological reflection, it cannot determine it. Yes, the person of Jesus has always been an element of the confession 'You are the Christ,' but ever since the emergence of a historical consciousness during the enlightenment and, more specifically, the quests for the historical Jesus, there has been a gap between the inherited theological claims and the historical referent himself. Regardless of how one understands the presence of God in the process of canonization and the ecumenical councils, its history is as human as Jesus. The bulk of this project will be determined by the tension between the following two elements within a constructive Christology, but the next chapter will address the historical Jesus and its role more directly.

When looking at the theological appropriation of contemporary Jesus research, I will outline a particular trajectory of liberal engagement with the historical Jesus that both affirms the existential reality of faith, the particularity of Jesus as its referent, and the negative norm that historical Jesus research can provide to constructive theology. Here it will be important to note how the historical Jesus' historicity is neither arbitrary for faith nor determinative for it. Second, I will briefly survey three different contemporary historical Jesus scholars: Elisabeth Schussler Fiorenza, Richard Horsley, and James Dunn. There I intend to highlight the current state of the quest and a few particular emphases to guide the task of constructive theology. Recognizing how an overwhelming majority of our historical material comes out of a confessional Christian community reflecting the church's own location as the living body of Christ, problematizing the initial dream of the quest itself. These texts contain a multiplicity of voices from the early churches and originate in a social matrix we are coming to know more and more about. Taken together, this means that the constructive theologian is invited not just to wrestle with the historical Jesus, but also recognize the situated nature of the texts in different communities and the communities' own sense of participation in God as mediated by Jesus, which imply that the hermeneutical terms for critical engagement have switched. While the historical endeavor cannot ultimately get behind the communal and confessional structure of the early church, it offers new constructive openings.

The Existential Register of Christology

A second element of the Christological conundrum is its existential shape. Kierkegaard's insight into the subjective character of the Christian confession cannot be sublated behind any form of objective certainty. No intellectual investigation into the identity of Jesus requires the confession that he is the Christ. The inability to demand the verdict is not a limitation of our current available evidence, the depravity of our culture, nor the giftedness of our apologists. Rightly, the liberal theological tradition has recognized the very nature of the claim itself rejects procedures of certainty. Peter's initial confession of Jesus brings this element to the fore. When Jesus poses the question to his disciples, "Who do people say that I am?" he is asking a valid question and receives answers that are justifiable responses. Both people who encountered Jesus or heard about Jesus had a diversity of legitimate responses to his ministry, each of which located Jesus within the horizon and expectations of their world. The typology of the answers the disciples reported were not specifically important, but the recognition that the existential response of a disciple's faith is not necessitated by an encounter or even by particular knowledge about Jesus. When Jesus asks Peter directly, "Who do you say that I am?" the form of the question is different. Jesus is not simply asking Peter to compare, contrast, or argue for a more valid assessment, but to make a statement of his fidelity. When Peter responds by saying, "You are the Christ, the Son of the living God," he is not making a statement that is the objective conclusion only he could draw because of his presence to the ministry of Jesus, for the other disciples too were present for the same events. What Peter is doing is making a confession of his faith, a response itself a response to the God who is present to him through Jesus. Jesus' response that his Father in heaven revealed this to him gives us an insight into just where this confession of Jesus as the Christ comes from. It is not a conclusion or even a verdict demanded by the evidence, but a confessional response to the God who was present in Christ. The response of Peter was fidelity, a fidelity full of risk, mystery, and demand. After all this is the nature of faith. The task for Peter, and for those of us seized and riddled by the Christ, is not to get Jesus' title correct, as if faith amounts to proper labeling. No, the task of the disciple is to understand the content of the confession and then begin the journey to inhabit that same mind that was in Christ Jesus. Peter may have received the identity of Jesus in faith, but he continually resisted the way of Christ all the way to the cross.

In the synoptic narrative, Peter's God-facilitated confession of faith was not a static one. It was not as if upon identifying Jesus as the Christ that he had in some sense arrived, and in fact, the narratives themselves get at the contested content of title itself. Setting Peter's confession in contrast to the denunciation he received from Jesus when he resisted Christ's mission to go to Jerusalem and to the cross, is essential for realizing the existential register of the confession. Peter responded to Jesus as the Christ, because of the work of the Father, and yet when Peter resisted the mission of Jesus he was denounced—"get behind me Satan!" The Christological problem these two vignettes demonstrate, which cohere with the larger synoptic narrative, is that the disciple's predicament is not the act of identifying Jesus as the Christ, but in coming to grips with affirming the mission of God and the character of the Christ. The problem of Peter the disciple was not one of identification, but rather of identifying with the mission of the Christ. Said another way, the Christological challenge is about the cost of discipleship and coming to grips with a Christ who turns toward Jerusalem and the cross. This is an existential challenge, for to stay with the Christ is to go toward the cross.

Returning to the role of historical Jesus scholarship in the task of Christology, the confession of Peter demonstrates that the identification of Jesus' messianic vocation is not a conclusion to be drawn from historical contemporaries of Jesus and thus it would be odd to think a historian could succeed in doing so. When it comes to the significant challenge the person of Jesus put to those who called him the Christ, the help of the historian serves a different role. Just as Peter sought to fill in the content of his confession with his own ideas and dreams for God and the kingdom, so too does each generation of disciples. Given the distance that contemporary Christians have with Jesus' historical situation, it should not be surprising that the same power at work in Peter who resisted Jesus' own mission would be at work in the church as well. Historical Jesus research is one of the most powerful tools for addressing the temptation to deny the missiological nature of the Christ-confession and resist the call of the one he called *Abba*.[1]

God and the Metaphysical Register

A third element that shapes contemporary Christology is the reality of God and God's relationship to the world. For much of church history, belief in God was a given and God's revelation in Jesus was more or less assumed. Today even the most verbose apologist or ardent atheist must acknowledge the plausibility of a different answer to the question of God.[2] In fact, the same stage from which

---

1. Historical Jesus research is not the only, or even the best, means to do this. One of the best lessons from the 20th century is the ideological blinders the West has put on its missiological imagination. The quest for the historical Jesus is not immune to this at all. The emergence of liberation theologies across the globe, many utilizing historical Jesus research outside the cultural privilege of the West, have been extremely rich contributors to this challenge.
2. Charles Taylor, *A Secular Age* (Cambridge, MA: The Belknap Press of Harvard University Press, 2007), 20-22.

the reality of God is debated is too often the same setting for Christological articulation. This sets the parameters for Christological affirmation to the terms of a publicly defensible understanding of God. How one understands the reality of God, the possibility of divine action, and the nature of divine revelation will dramatically affect one's Christology.

The questions and challenges that the tradition encounters today cannot be finally answered. We must leave them open and carried into the theological project itself.[3] That seems to be the minimal viable acknowledgement of our conditions.[4] The problem, however, with a methodologically weighted Christology is significant. Christological confessions made within the limits of reason alone may end higher than expected, but have a hard time shaking the detachment and self-possession the method employs. One would hardly count it a success if Peter had answered Jesus' question, "Who do they say that I am?" with "Some say Elijah, others John the Baptist, and still others an apocalyptic prophet of God's Kingdom or a wandering cynic-sage known for practicing open table fellowship, and yet others a probable Son of God to be vindicated by resurrection from the dead." One cannot put a Christology in the form of a report no more than a sonnet into a syllogism. It is contained within the very shape of a Christological confession that one is not only identifying just how God was present in the person of Jesus, but is also talking about God with one's very self up for grabs.

Christology is not a spectator doctrine. To call Jesus the Christ is an enactment of the entire person in a particular community. Reflection upon this confession is not something one can do from a distance, because the confession itself entails an existential response that requires much more than the affirmation of beliefs. Christology is a disciple's discipline. What the evidence does not and cannot give is the response that is the beginning point of all Christological reflection. This response is not evidential, but existential. It is not demanded, but gifted. The response of faith, should we take Jesus' own assessment of such a confession seriously, does not come from anything in this world. Contingent existence in all its glory could not bear witness to the infinite

---

3. Wolfhart Pannenberg, *Systematic Theology*, trans. Geoffrey W. Bromiley, vol. 1 (Göttingen, Germany: Vandenhoeck & Ruprecht, 1988; Waco, TX: Eerdmans, 2010), 107-8. Citations refer to the Eerdmans edition.

4. Wesley J. Wildman, *Fidelity with Plausibility: Modest Christologies in the Twentieth Century* (Albany, NY: State University of New York Press, 1998).

2

THE JESUS OF HISTORY FOR THE CONTEMPORARY DISCIPLE

"What did God do in Christ that we couldn't do for ourselves?" I posed that question to a group of prestigious progressive American theologians. The question was simple. It was submitted and selected online by interested laypeople, hoping these theologians could assist and inspire them in their own theological reflection. Answers ranged between the heavy nuancing of traditional language, a rejection of the question's conditions, or a simple 'nothing.' What became clear is that both those in the pew and in the academy wrestle to articulate vibrant and viable theological responses to age-old questions. The question given to the theologians makes several assumptions; that God acted in Christ and that God's action in Christ does something beyond the potential of the person prior to God's action. These assumptions, among others, are not striking in the context of the Church's Christological conversations and yet they are problematic enough that it was both a popular question among the laity and a difficult question to answer for the theologians.

Since the beginning of the enlightenment, the intellectual conversation in the West has developed at an expedient pace both vertically and horizontally. The sheer volume of information and data that has been collected, developed, and established, dwarfs the rest of human history with ease. In addition, those who have access and familiarity with the 'fruits of our learning' is expanding. Literacy is no longer a privilege of the elites and access to the entire history and development of traditions is just a few clicks away. This context affects theological thinking in a variety of ways, but most forcefully, it democratizes and then relativizes the authority of the church and its tradition. For Christology, the conversation not only includes a whole host of lay people reading the Gospels, but also Dan Brown. A world with Dan Brown on the bestsellers' list is one where not only the tradition of the Church is suspect, but where there is enough general awareness of legitimate challenges to its authority that they become speculative material for fiction. Between the History, Discovery, and National Geographic channels on cable, more and more people are facing the cognitive dissonance of a faith facing the challenge of science and the quest for the historical Jesus in a world of unimaginable religious diversity. These three challenges extend way beyond an hour-long special during Holy Week on the life of Jesus. It is these realities and the courage to face them that makes it difficult for a theologian to answer simply the question, "What did God do in Christ that we couldn't do for ourselves?"

Exploring Christology in the light of history, science, and religious pluralism, is difficult but should it be debilitating? Any of these intellectual pursuits can appear debilitating at this point in the enlightenment. Surely, some forms of Christology developed in the past cannot speak persuasively today. Yet over the course of the enlightenment, the church and its theologians have felt its authority slip away as we gained more knowledge with an ever-widening distribution. Responses to the situation have varied greatly. Some theologians have rejected the challenges by discussing theological methodology to create a space wherein they could continue the church's dogmatics. Others have invested themselves apologetically against one or more of these challenges to demonstrate the sustainability of tradition. Yet for those that opened themselves up to these new sources of information, just how they function in one's theologizing was not immediately obvious. As the West became more smitten with these intellectual discourses, for the more open and liberal theologians, they came to serve as new enlightenment solas and framed the possibilities for a viable theology. This decision is wrought with a difficulty beyond simply comprehending a new field. As academic disciplines, science and history are largely agnostic or worse for claims of divine revelation or action. Commenting on this issue, Paul Minear said, "History has become the rolling up of the carpet after the procession has passed, with little regard for the nature of the procession or the marchers."[1] When the authority and limits of any discipline or a required conclusion about religious pluralism is determined *a priori* of specifically Christian reflection, they are operating like the solas of the Reformation, except

---

1. Paul Minear, "Gospel History: Celebration or Reconstruction," in *Jesus and Man's Hope*, ed. Donald G. Miller and Dikran Y. Hadidian, vol. 2 (Pittsburgh, PA: Pittsburgh Theological Seminary, 1971), 23.

that these frames for theological thinking are not native to the faith. To address this situation, an alternative approach to Christological methodology will be discussed so that the challenges faced no longer require a prolegomena, but are seen as integral to its outworking. The affirmation that 'in Christ God is reconciling the world to Godself is not something the historian or scientist will establish, even in his own time people wondered 'by what power does he do these things?' and yet that does not make the science and metaphysics of divine action any less important. What it points out is the need for what Michael Welker calls a "multi-systematic, polycontextual way of thinking" in which different rationalities and symbol systems are appreciated and discovered through bridge-building and ever-evolving universal theories.[2] It is essential that these universal theories be plural, not because there is more than one reality, but because finality will not be established under finite conditions and one's situated location cannot be universally transcended.[3] Positively put, it permits Christology to be a particular conversation with a universal horizon, one that should not ignore the larger truth-seeking conversation while also not inverting the movement by imposing universal stipulations on a particular experience from the outset. Said another way, Christology is a disciple's dogma and it can more authentically engage in the broader conversation when it owns its own identity.

In the past, this image of a disciple on a search for truth could be hard to justify. The wedding of Darwinism and genetic determinism, for example, created a context in which to self-identify as a disciple was to exit the serious conversation among the scientific community. That is no longer the case. This form of scientism no longer holds sway in its own community and need not for the disciple. In a similar way, the historian has functioned as a possibility-determining authority for the theological community. The combination of an optimistic historian's Jesus and the doctrine of the incarnation have led theologians to many Christs. This creates quite the pickle for the theologian hoping to talk about Christ, especially when there is an assumption an accessible historical Jesus as initiator of the faith is being explicated. What, then, is the

---

2. Michael Welker, "Who is Jesus Christ for Us Today?" *Harvard Theological Review* 95, no. 2 (2002): 129-130.

3. Clearly different discourses of a multi-systematic polycontextual way of thinking will be more or less situationally bounded. Science is an example of one less bounded.

theologian to do? Rely on the dated scholarship they learned as graduate students? Skim through the contemporary field as amateurs? Pick one's favorite and not so surprisingly complementary historical Jesus? Ignore the quest entirely? None of these options seem reasonable. We cannot go back to a world prior to historical criticism, but neither complete dependence nor independence will work today.[4] At this point, the hermeneutical stance of the disciple offers a possible way forward because it does not require historical justification at the outset, but remains committed to its endeavor. What is perhaps most intriguing is that the movement through the third quest for the historical Jesus opens up an exegetical stance to Jesus and the New Testament that moves beyond this impasse. Even more surprising is the claim that precisely the epistemological freedom gained through the advent of historical- critical consciousness, combined with the many quests for the Historical Jesus' inability to deliver a final account of the Jesus of history, which opens up a new space for a liberal and liberating Christ of faith.

The Quest's Liberation of Jesus

From its infancy, the liberal theological tradition has had a vested interest in the results of historical criticism.[5] Through appropriating the Enlightenment's commitment to autonomous reason, the many quests for the historical Jesus were always of interest for individual theologians seeking to articulate an intelligible Christology for their time. It would be inaccurate to assume, however, that the liberal tradition believed Christian theology to depend on the results of the historian.[6] As Kathryn Tanner notes, for Schleiermacher, "everything that a theologian needs to know about Jesus can be derived from the nature of Christian piety itself."[7] On into the twentieth century, Rudolf Bultmann and Paul Tillich continued a liberal suspicion of the theological

---

4. Dale C. Allison, *The Historical Christ and the Theological Jesus* (Grand Rapids, MI: Eerdmans, 2009), 14.

5. Friedrich Schleiermacher, *The Life of Jesus*, ed. Jack C. Verheyden, trans. S.M. Gilmour (Philadelphia: Fortress, 1975).

6. Historian of liberal theology Gary Dorrien has a shorthand definition that is appropriate here: "Theology based on reason and critically interpreted religious experience." Gary Dorrien, "American Liberal Theology: Crisis, Irony, Decline, Renewal, Ambiguity," *Cross Currents* 55, no. 4 (Winter 2006): 456-81.

7. Kathryn Tanner, "Jesus Christ," in *The Cambridge Companion to Christian Doctrine,* ed. Colin E. Gunton (Cambridge: Cambridge University Press, 1997), 258.

weight in the historian's results. Tillich noted how the theological investment in history created anxiety for both theologians and laity alike, and that it was rather participation in the New Being of Christ that brought faith, not history. He argued emphatically "historical research can neither give nor take away the foundation of the Christian faith" because of the very nature of faith.[8] Tillich, like Schleiermacher before him, embraced the use of reason and the reality of our historical consciousness that developed in the Enlightenment, but rejected founding religion and Christianity in particular on either the authority of the received tradition or a strict rationalism.

The subjective nature of faith that the liberal theological tradition has so cherished is threatened by both dogmatism and rationalism alike because both seek after external grounding for one's own identity in Christ. Contingent events of history serving as sources for absolute eternal truths were not necessarily more trustworthy than the tradition in question itself. Because the liberal theological tradition was born in the Enlightenment, it need not be forgotten that it protested a wholesale substitution of the tradition with reason. The ever-popular pitting of the Jesus of History against the Christ of Faith is not necessitated in liberal theology. More than setting the framework for the constructive proposal, the quest for the historical Jesus represented a justification for envisioning no longer the rigid repetition of past conclusions as faithfulness to the living tradition. For the liberal theologian, the Word of the Creed, like the Jesus of History, can both empower and hinder a passionate articulation of the Christ of Faith. So in the following discussion of the results and situation after the questers, one need not assume a vibrant liberal Christology always necessitates an established history. What was gained through the advent of historical-critical consciousness, despite the content of its returns, is a non-authoritarian methodology that cuts across the Protestant-Catholic divide. The liberal appropriation of the historical Jesus gave the theologian a seemingly unquestionable source to ground their rejection of scripture and the tradition as exclusive, but how it can contribute positively to a constructive Christology is up for debate.[9]

How more liberal theologians came to have a vested interest in the constructive possibilities out of quest for the historical Jesus is an important

---

8. Paul Tillich, *Systematic Theology*, vol. 2 (Chicago: University of Chicago Press, 1957), 113.
9. Tillich discusses how he tentatively can use the historical results positively on Ibid., 105-7.

development. Gerhard Ebeling, one of Bultmann's students, sought to clarify the function of historical criticism for liberal theology by distinguishing the theologian's view of history from that of the historian. Bultmann argued that we cannot know anything about the life of the historical Jesus, nor should the gospel proclamation need such a verification. Rather than making the hermeneutical observation that the historical Jesus is a construction of the historian based on the evidence at hand, Ebeling thought Bultmann had too strongly tied the 'historical Jesus' to the actual first century Jew who lived, preached, and was crucified.[10] Ebeling thought the liberal theological commitment should distinguish the historicist view of history from the diaconal view taken by the Christian theologian. The historicist view focuses overwhelmingly on the reconstruction of the past, yet when all the past is historicized, the past is no longer one's tradition, but something to be researched. History becomes an object. When the self becomes an object and product of history, one ceases to look within one's self, thus short-circuiting the connection between the individual as a self before God. In the historicist view, there is no longer a way to step outside the construction of history. For Ebeling, the kerygma leads one to view Christ in a diaconal view in which one listens and responds to the past with an attitude of submission and a readiness to be transformed in the present.[11] He thought this modification of Bultmann's insistence preserved the liberal theological commitment to the subjective nature of faith while recognizing that the early church's confession of Jesus as the Christ suggests a historical event. The kerygma itself pushes one toward asking the historical question in a historical age, but like those in a previous 'metaphysical age,' comprehending and articulating the event is not tantamount or even necessarily related to the event of experiencing Jesus as the Christ. For example, one can understand the predicate 'the Christ' historically without offense. It is in the application of the Christological predicates to the person of Jesus that a claim is made.[12] The early church was applying these predicates to the person of Jesus to give explanatory or substantive content to the person of Jesus. Today, in light of the historical consciousness embodied in our contemporary ethos, one must do this in

---

10. Gerhard Ebeling, *Theology and Proclamation: Dialogue with Bultmann,* trans. John Riches (Philadelphia: Fortress, 1966), 33-36.

11. Ibid., 17.

12. Ibid., 49-50.

reverse.[13] One cannot simply discuss the predicates but return to the event where these predicates are applied to a person while recognizing that such historical investigations and their conclusions are not the essence of faith. For Ebeling, identifying a historical event as an act of God is not a historian's job but a theologian's, because the identification is of a predicate in the historical event that likewise involves the predication of the self, world, etc.

Ebeling's liberal trajectory is not the only one that ends up committed but not ultimately determined by historical investigations. One need only think of the rippling influence of Pannenberg's Christology: *Jesus: God and Man*, to recognize that the question of history could no longer be ignored by Bultmannians and Barthians alike.[14] For those who dare to attempt a constructive liberal Christology, Ebeling's moves appear normative, and are echoed by Peter Hodgson. Hodgson argues that historical investigation helps uncover the contextual particularity of the Christ event, while admitting, "We start with the present experience of this figure as alive and at work in the world," which helps both interpret the history and shatter it simultaneously.[15] Ebeling's appropriation of the liberal tradition makes a few observations that are assumed today in many forms.[16] First, our contemporary context in the West does not permit the church to ignore the questions raised by the historians. The contemporary consciousness is historical.[17] Second, the rise of historical consciousness supports the liberal critique of authoritarian religion in which the

---

13. Ibid., 75.

14. Pannenberg states his thesis strongly when he says, "Jesus possesses significance 'for us' only to the extent that this significance is inherent in himself, in his history, and in his person constituted by this history. Only when this can be shown may we be sure that we are not merely attaching our questions, wishes, and thoughts to this figure. Therefore, Christology, the question about Jesus himself, about his person, as he lived on earth in the time of Emperor Tiberius, must remain prior to all questions about his significance, to all soteriology. Soteriology must follow from Christology, not vice versa. Otherwise, faith in salvation itself loses a real foundation." Wolfhart Pannenberg, *Jesus - God and Man*, trans. Lewis L. Wilkins and Duane A. Priebe, 2nd ed. (Philadelphia: Westminster, 1968), 48. This statement though stronger, shares the same sentiment of Ebeling's critique of Bultmann's failure to recognize the necessity of the historical question when he says, "The theological intention of talk about the That of God, is that it should be confessed and believed in relation to the What and the How of historic reality." Gerhard Ebeling, *Theology and Proclamation: Dialogue with Bultmann*, trans. John Riches (Philadelphia: Fortress, 1966), 69.

15. Peter Hodgson, *Winds of the Spirit: A Constructive Christian Theology* (Louisville, KY: Westminster John Knox, 1994), 232-33.

16. These points Ebeling developed in contrast to his mentor Bultmann represent the liberal heritage that can be seen in many contemporary theologians including Roger Haight, Douglas Ottati, Hans Kung, Jürgen Moltmann, John Cobb, and Elizabeth Johnson.

17. See Roger Haight's discussion of this in Catholic thought in Haight, *The Future of Christology* (New York: Continuum, 2007), 13-31.

Christian faith is determined or bound by external markers of dogma. Third, the historian's conversation about the historical Jesus is consequential to the theologian's work, but the historical Jesus is not the object of faith.[18] Elizabeth Johnson, a liberal Catholic theologian, echoes this sentiment when she states that:

> The image of the historical Jesus, formed by the coalescence of historical knowledge about him, is not properly utilized if it becomes a verification or proof of faith. It is, however, theologically relevant for faith because it gives concrete content to the faith confession, corrects faith images of Jesus, and, most crucially, carries the element of the free, divine 'given' in the Christ event, the actuality of God's self-gift in history to which Christian faith is a response.[19]

Last, the results of the quest for the historical Jesus function as a negative norm. A constructive Christological proposal cannot dismiss or exclude essential identity markers of Jesus. For example, a Christology that affirms the full humanity of Jesus cannot fail to recognize the full Jewishness of Jesus.[20] Some liberal theologians, like Roger Haight, extend this negative norm such that "one cannot affirm of Jesus what is positively excluded by a consensus of history."[21] Here one can run into the hermeneutical limitations of history as a discipline and their ever-elusive 'consensus.'

Third Quest Consensus?

Deciphering the different quests for the historical Jesus is as confusing as attempting to draw consensus conclusions from the many quests' unique journeys. For example, what is deemed in many quarters the Third Quest can also be deemed the ninth distinct quest by another historian's count.[22] If both publishing and presentations at guild meetings are any indications, there is a lull in grand proposals today, yet this lull is not marked by a clarity in many details. For this essay's investigation of the liberal theological tradition's constructive

---

18. Neither is a docetic or monophysite Christology, both of which are eliminated when the historical Jesus is part of the constructive proposal.

19. Elizabeth A. Johnson, "The Theological Relevance of the Historical Jesus: A Debate and a Thesis," *The Thomist* 48 (1984): 35.

20. That the Kingdom of God was Jesus' dominant message and that he understood God in a uniquely Abba-intimate way would also be examples.

21. Ibid., 30.

22. Clive Marsh, "Quests of the Historical Jesus in New Historicist Perspective," *Biblical Interpretation* 5 (1997): 404-37.

appropriation of contemporary research, two different accounts need to be noted: both the academic story of the field's development, and the theological questions being raised along the way.[23]

What has the third quest for the historical Jesus brought us? For one thing, it is not clarity. N.T. Wright, the scholar who coined the term 'third quest,' has found that the phrase itself was picked up without the boundary markers he drew, but despite the lack of a clear consensus on the third quest's makeup, there are certain things that are consistently identified with it. In the late 1940s, the discovery of the Dead Sea Scrolls at Qumran and the Nag Hammadi library in Egypt opened scholars' eyes to ancient communities that had previously been known only through their opponents. The apocalyptic community of Qumran, and Gnostic texts from Nag Hammadi, pushed scholars to reassess their view of the first century religious matrix of Jesus and the early church.

Most descriptions of the third quest highlight the role of E.P. Sanders and the Jesus Seminar in shaping the contours of the conversation.[24] The Jesus Seminar was a conglomerate of New Testament scholars notorious for their bead work, which attempted to establish the historical veracity of the sayings and deeds of the historical Jesus. As Borg likes to highlight, they were the first "collaborative systematic examination of the entire Jesus tradition ever undertaken, unprecedented in the history of scholarship."[25] The seminar's opponents were quick to point out the unprecedented efficiency of their publicists.[26] The group itself was not homogenous, but it consistently produced a non-apocalyptic Jesus. It was optimistic about some Gnostic contributions' historicity and found the strongest historical parallel to Jesus in the wandering Cynic sage. In the opposite corner, E.P. Sanders' groundbreaking work *Jesus and Judaism* argued forcefully that Jesus must be positioned between first century Judaism and the early church.[27] This methodological starting point does two things. First, it emphasizes the Jewishness of Jesus and the early

---

23. It is interesting that both Marcus Borg in *Jesus in Contemporary Scholarship* and N.T. Wright in *Jesus and the Victory of God* see both of these thought streams taking unique shape in the Third Quest.

24. John Meier, "The Present State of the 'Third Quest' for the Historical Jesus: Loss and Gain," *Biblica* 80, no. 4 (1999): 459-87.

25. Marcus Borg, *Jesus in Contemporary Scholarship* (Harrisburg, PA: Trinity International, 1994), 6.

26. Luke Timothy Johnson, *The Real Jesus: The Misguided Quest for the Historical Jesus and the Truth of the Traditional Gospels* (San Francisco: Harper One, 1997).

27. E.P Sanders, *Jesus and Judaism* (Philadelphia: Fortress, 1985), 18-22.

church, not allowing the shape of post-Temple Christianity to determine what is and is not historically possible. For Sanders then, conclusions with a stronger coherence between the Judaism that nourished Jesus and the first post-Easter communities are privileged. This conclusion of Sanders' conflicts most strongly with the seminar's Burton Mack, whose Jesus is "neither eschatological nor very Jewish."[28] Second, Sanders' perspective gave interpretive priority to the 'virtually certain' details of Jesus' life and particularly those explanations that explain how his ministry could cause his death.[29] One such conclusion is his emphasis on Jesus' apocalyptic preaching in contrast to the Jesus Seminar. For Sanders, continuing the thesis of the previous quest's strongest voice, Albert Schweitzer, "Jesus is to be positively connected with the hope for Jewish restoration."[30] In doing so, Sanders eliminates the possibility to "shift the normal expectations of Jewish restoration theology to the periphery." Thus, Sanders has determined a few secure conclusions in his mind, primarily that: "Jesus expected the kingdom in the near future, he awaited the rebuilding of the temple, he called 'twelve' to symbolize the restoration of Israel, and his disciples thought about the kingdom concretely enough to ask about their place in it."[31]

Interestingly, when figures within the debate give their accounts of the developments of the latest quest's results, they part ways along battle lines. Marcus Borg and N.T. Wright give two compelling and divergent views of Jesus. Despite sharing a dissertation advisor and maintaining a friendship, their conclusions are desperately different, as seen in their co-authored and bestselling book *The Meaning of Jesus: Two Visions*.[32] When Borg gives an account of the three features of the 'renaissance in Jesus studies', he highlights: (1) the erosion of Schweitzer's hypothesis that Jesus was an apocalyptic prophet, (2) the recognition that Jesus was historically a teacher of subversive wisdom, and (3) the necessity of placing Jesus within the social world he inhabited.[33] The strikingly new insights of Borg's account are not so groundbreaking in Wright's mind. He finds their continued over-reliance on the

---

28. Borg, *Jesus in Contemporary Scholarship*, 21.

29. Sanders, *Jesus and Judaism*, 326-27.

30. Ibid., 118.

31. Ibid., 156.

32. Marcus Borg and N.T. Wright, *The Meaning of Jesus: Two Visions* (San Francisco: HarperCollins, 2000).

33. Borg, *Jesus in Contemporary Scholarship*, 9-12.

sayings material and their assessment through various criteria a "spurious idea" for a historian.[34] For Wright, the seminar's trajectory originated out of the "thoroughgoing skepticism" of William Wrede rather than the "thoroughgoing eschatology" of Schweitzer.[35] This skepticism justifies Borg and company to divorce the sayings of Jesus from the narrative in which they are found and the thoroughly Jewish context of Jesus and the early church.[36] Wright's criticism consistently takes this skepticism to task for being unsustainable in light of the seminar's proposals. For example, in response to connecting Jesus' social identification most closely to that of the cynics, Wright questions, "What he totally fails to explain is why this Cynic teacher should have started a movement that so quickly spread throughout the known world, with results significantly different from those either of Cynicism as a whole or any particular Cynic teacher."[37] Wright, in a move toward sharp contrast, identifies the third quest as having a single operating assumption, namely that Jesus is to be placed "precisely within his Jewish eschatological context."[38]

Despite these differences, one notices two strong similarities in both of their projects that have today become more popular in the academy; namely that the ministry of Jesus was intended and understood to contain a challenge to Roman imperialism, and that the eschatological language employed by Jesus was not intended to be taken literally.[39] Wright and Borg's ongoing discussion has changed the terrain of historical Jesus scholarship. Early on, it was a more robust academic battle, focusing on the legitimacy of the Gospel of Thomas as an early source or the viability of the criterion of dissimilarity, but as their intellectual sparring continued, the theological investment in their historical accounts came to the surface. If one looks at their publishing track records, this historical stalemate was followed by both of them writing accounts of their theological visions, interpretations of scriptures, and understandings of Christian ethics for a general audience. In an essay reflecting on the progress of the newest shape of the quest, Borg identified the theological question fueling

---

34. N.T. Wright, *Jesus and the Victory of God* (Minneapolis, MN: Fortress, 1996), 79.

35. Wright, *Victory of God*, 28.

36. Borg and Wright, *Meaning of Jesus,* 23.

37. Wright, *Victory of God,* 73.

38. Wright, *Victory of God*, 81.

39. In my personal conversations with them, I was surprised how they both acknowledged these two similarities—especially the eschatological point, given what the non-literal language intends is strikingly different.

the interest as "the question of continuity or discontinuity between the historical Jesus and the proclamation of the early church."[40] Both scholarly churchmen answer this question differently, and yet their answers take the same shape. Their own account of the historical Jesus gives rise to their account of the early church, and is their impetus behind the 'heart' of what it means to be 'simply' Christian.[41]

Through the 80s and 90s, this third quest raged not just in the scholarly world, but also in the public square.[42] At the turn of the century, there had been no unanimous declarations from the 'historical Jesus study group' of the SBL. And as all the new data has worked its way through the academy, there developed a lull in the grand proposals and attention turned rather to detailed analysis of particular issues.[43] Powell, chair of the historical Jesus studies section of SBL, notes that the field is coming into its own. It is ceasing to segment the quest into periods and instead sees itself "as a progressive process of often insightful exploration."[44] In his reflection on the future of historical Jesus studies, he notes current patterns such as less reliance on apocryphal gospels, a new cautious use of John as a historical source, a resurgence of orthodoxy, a dethroning of dissimilarity as a dominant criterion for authenticity, and an increase in the attribution of some form of messianic consciousness to the historical Jesus.[45] In reference to the divergence of Sanders and the Seminar, Powell notes that today, "there is a marked return to the idea that Jesus proclaimed an eschatological/apocalyptic message of a coming kingdom."[46] The Jesus Seminar's proposal has not been eliminated, but now remains as a "moderately persuasive case for what has become a minority understanding."[47]

---

40. Borg, *Jesus in Contemporary Scholarship*, 6.
41. Here I am referring to Marcus Borg's *The Heart of Christianity* and N. T. Wright's *Simply Christian* as exemplifying the theological fruit and impetus of their work.
42. For a wonderful summary of the field, see Helen Bond, *The Historical Jesus: A Guide for the Perplexed* (London: T & T Clark International, 2012).
43. Mark Allan Powell, "'Things That Matter': Historical Jesus Studies in the New Millennium," *Word & World* 29, no. 2 (Spring 2009): 121-28.
44. Ibid., 123.
45. Ibid., 122-26.
46. Ibid., 127.
47. Ibid., 123.

Continued Questing Possibilities

For those who hoped finally to get a consensus on the historical Jesus, the time has not yet come, if there will ever be such a time.[48] Perhaps one could attempt to make a summary statement of the dominant depiction in the academy, but even as one states it, there are other viable interpretations waiting in the wing.[49] It is hard to imagine arriving at a viable candidate for historical Jesus when knowing both the prevalent anachronism of the past questers and the diversity in the present questers. As Paula Fredriksen rightly commented, "a truly 'historical' Jesus can be no less constituted by his historical, social, and cultural circumstances than we are."[50] While the current situation within historical Jesus studies has honed its focus to the sifting of details in a heterogeneous community, the different depictions of where the work is taking place reveals a theologically permissive shift. Take, for example, the goals for the historian through the quests. The first quest sought to write lives of Jesus and was chastened for it. Then there was a search to uncover the bare facts of his history in both the definite sayings and the secure actions of Jesus.[51] The conclusions were often arranged and interpreted toward the conclusions the historian or on looking theologian desired.[52] It was, however, in this search for facts that the scholarly community became increasingly aware of two important conclusions

---

48. Dale Allison said that "the unification of academic opinion would be almost as miraculous as the union of the churches. If you are holding your breath waiting for the consensus of the specialists, you will pass out." Dale C. Allison Jr., *The Historical Christ and the Theological Jesus* (Grand Rapids, MI: Eerdmans, 2009), 11.

49. John Meier gives what amounts to a reasonably accurate image of the dominant consensus post-third quest when he describes Jesus as a "Jew who proclaimed the present yet future kingdom, who was also an itinerant prophet and miracle worker in the guise of Elijah, who was also a teacher and interpreter of the Mosaic Law, who was also a charismatic leader who called disciples to follow him at great price, who was also a religious personage whose perceived messianic claims wound up getting him crucified by the Roman prefect, in the end, a crucified religious figure who was soon proclaimed by his followers as risen from the dead and Lord of all." Meier, "The Present State," 478.

50. Paula Fredriksen, "What Does Jesus Have to Do with Christ? What Does Knowledge Have to Do with Faith? What Does History Have to Do with Theology?" in *Christology: Memory, Inquiry, Practice* ed. Anne M. Clifford and Anthony J. Godzieba, College Theology Society Annual Volume no. 48 (Maryknoll, NY: Orbis Books, 2003), 8.

51. The seven appendices in Crossan's major work are a good example of this type of work. John Dominic Crossan, *The Historical Jesus: The Life of a Mediterranean Jewish Peasant* (New York: HarperCollins, 1992), 427-66.

52. William Loader, "Finding Faith in Fact and Fiction: Making Sense of the New Testament While Maintaining Our Integrity and The Integrity of the Text," *Colloquium* 40, no. 1 (2008): 23-27.

that can steer the present interpreter away from placing the facts like pearls on their own string.

First, it has become increasingly clear that despite the discoveries of the twentieth century, the primary sources for credible material connected to the historical Jesus are the canonical gospels themselves.[53] Even the minority of scholars who date the gospel of Thomas early have little if any context for interpreting or assessing the attested sayings without turning to the canonical Gospels. As it has become clear that no historical tool can take the quester behind the Gospels to the historical Jesus, the turn is then to seek him in and through the Gospels. It is important to note that the Gospels are not univocal taken either individually or as a whole, nor are they of equal historical assessment. The point is simply that for now, beyond a few sentences from an outsider that could affirm knowledge of Jesus' existence, ministry, death, and the testimony of the early church, the historian is working with insider information - namely the Gospels.[54]

The second methodological transition in the quest is the recognition of the contextually embedded nature of the texts, events, peoples, and accounts of Jesus. Initially, this came to the fore as our understanding of first century Judaism developed through the new discoveries of the twentieth century. Having a much more robust depiction of Jesus' world with its multiplicity of Judaisms and an awareness of the socio-political context of his day, scholars began to eliminate hypotheses that did not embed Jesus in his world. But beyond the historical embedding is the recognition that there is no unembedded historical figure. To develop a historical Jesus that is self-sufficient would be to develop a Jesus without a history. We can no longer assume that he can be completely detached from the experience of him by his first followers, their memories, post-Easter experiences, and retellings.[55] Clearly all the experiences of the disciples were not homogenous, but they share something that differentiates them from the rest of those Jesus encountered in his life. To be

---

53. Meier, "The Present State," 464-67. See also James D. G. Dunn, *Jesus Remembered: Christianity in the Making* (Grand Rapids, MI: Eerdmans, 2003), 139-72.
54. The outsider remarks I am thinking of are the brief and debated statement of Josephus. The mentions of Pliny the Younger and Tacitus are better seen as historical awareness of the early church's testimony.
55. Francis Watson makes a similar observation and then develops a theological account of the "dynamics of reception" in the early church. See Watson, "Veritas Christi," in *Seeking the Identity of Jesus: A Pilgrimage,* ed. Beverly Roberts Gaventa & Richard B. Hays (Grand Rapids, MI: Eerdmans, 2008), 105-13.

sure, there were those who ignored him, never heard of him, assailed him, were intrigued by him, forgot about him, associated him with other contemporary and past figures, and some who thought he was trouble from Satan. And yet, the Gospel accounts from which we gain most of our information about Jesus identified him as the Christ. Should those other groups have recorded their responses, they would have varied greatly, and the historian can be both aware of the subjective nature of the reports and shift the dominant interpretive stance. Instead of reading the Gospels primarily to establish an objective history, our historical knowledge of the context, can facilitate a more responsible reading of the texts. The history we do know facilitates a more attentive reading of the historical testimony of the Gospels. The highly probable facts in which there is a strong consensus, like those listed by E.P. Sanders above, can function as interpretive controls. You could describe the shift as a move away from an archeological perspective in which the Gospel texts are seen like a dig site, and mostly as debris that needs to be discarded to get to the few artifacts of objective history.

The Quest for Jesus beyond the Limits of History Alone

From these two methodological transitions, there has been a turn toward the narratives and their communities, which have become the two most stable partners for the historian. What this approach looks like differs and the conclusions even more so, yet what is essential to note is the transition toward prioritizing the remembered Jesus. The spectrum of those sharing this methodological approach includes people from Larry Hurtado[56] to Richard

---

56. Hurtado, *Lord Jesus Christ: Devotion to Jesus in Earliest Christianity* (Grand Rapids, MI: Eerdmans, 2003).

Horsley,[57] and from Elizabeth Schussler Fiorenza[58] to James D.G. Dunn.[59] A brief look at two of these figures demonstrates how they are reshaping the historian's approach to the texts.

Richard Horsley's criticism of traditional historical Jesus studies developed out of his own examination of the non-bifurcated relationship of religion and politics in first century Palestine. In Jesus' historical context, such sharp a distinction would not have been drawn, but the academic community has received these texts in a context where religion and the state are much more distinct.[60] Through a socio-historical analysis of the Gospels, Horsley could identify the hidden transcripts of resistance in the texts. What he identifies as 'hidden' was arguably much less subtle in its native historical context. What he discovered were Gospels in which the narrative itself is a performative oral work of the community for its historical context.[61] For example, Horsley sees the Gospel of Mark as portraying Jesus and his movement as part of a subjugated people, who, while rooted in the history of Israel, claim that this movement is the fulfillment of that people's history.[62] The notion of a 'people's history' is a noticeable departure from the quest for a historical Jesus. In Horsley's mind, future research must see the Gospels as orally derived, performed, fluid, and contextually embedded texts. In contrast to the

---

57. Horsley, *Jesus in Context: Power, People, and Performance* (Minneapolis, MN: Fortress, 2008); Horsley, *Hearing the Whole Story: The Politics of the Plot in Mark's Gospel* (Louisville, KY: Westminster John Knox, 2001).

58. Fiorenza, *Jesus: Miriam's Child, Sophia's Prophet* (New York: Continuum, 1995); Fiorenza, *In Memory of Her: A Feminist Theological Reconstruction of Christian Origins* (New York: Crossroads Publishing, 1994). Of particular interest for documenting the transition is the essential role of memory and remembering. For example, Fiorenza writes, "To understand Jesus research as a critical practice of remembering... rather than as a quest for certainties, engenders a shift from a rhetoric of scientific or theological positivism that seeks to produce scientific certainty to one that aims at critical retrieval and articulation of memory. Memory and remembering as a reconstructive frame of meaning do not require one to construe a dualistic opposition between history and theology, objectivity and interestedness, Jesus and Judaism, Jesus the exceptional individual and Jesus shaped by his community; between the pre-Easter Jesus and the post-Easter Jesus, the historical Jesus and the kerygmatic Christ." Fiorenza, *Jesus and Politics of Interpretation* (New York: Continuum, 2000), 75.

59. Dunn, *Jesus Remembered.*

60. Horsley, *Jesus in Context,* 16-17. See also his early, paradigm shifting work, *Jesus and the Spiral of Violence: Popular Jewish Resistance in Roman Palestine* (Minneapolis, MN: Fortress, 1987).

61. Horsley develops his analysis of Mark in his book *Hearing the Whole Story.* There he states that "once we peel away unwarranted historical assumptions, it becomes clear that Mark is telling a story about people's history, a history that had been previously submerged under the weight of the dominant Roman imperial order." Richard A. Horsley, *Hearing the Whole Story: The Politics of Plot in Mark's Gospel* (Louisville, KY: Westminster John Knox, 2001), 44.

62. Ibid., 44-47.

archeological approach to the text that searches for data, "it seems that investigators of the historical Jesus must become bona fide Gospel scholars, pursuing the full range of approaches to the Gospels, the sources in which an irreducibly relational Jesus is embedded." [63] There have been criticisms leveled against Horsley for letting his 'people's history' be overly political, but regardless of whether this is a legitimate criticism, it is clear that Horsley points a way forward, which in recognition of the Gospels' oral and communal nature supports his advocacy for a more relational approach to the study of both the Gospels and the historical Jesus. These two categories will no longer be clear and distinct for, "what matters in a performed text is not so much what it means on its own, as the work it does on and in the community of hearers."[64]

James Dunn's work also demonstrates the character of this new approach. He describes the methodological shift as a change in the default settings from understanding the texts as literary constructions to transcriptions of the early church's oral performances.[65] What Dunn makes clear is how incompatible the traditional quest's treatment of the texts are with how they were composed. In Dunn's intensive study, *Jesus Remembered*, he explores the evidence for a relatively normative Jesus tradition that was shared by churches, and how the Gospels themselves demonstrate a "lively interest among the first Christians in knowing about Jesus, in preserving, promoting, and defending the memory of his mission and in learning from his example."[66] For Dunn, his sociological and socio-anthropological analysis of group formation patterns leads him to say that the early Jesus movement, "almost certainly [would] have required a foundation story (or stories) to explain, to themselves as well as others, why they had formed."[67] There is then a real, substantive continuity between Jesus and the early church within Dunn's mind, and likewise a barrier for moving beyond these texts as performative for "each telling is a performance of the tradition" and not a composition of it.[68] The interpreter, should they take

---

63. Horsley, *Jesus in Context*, 228 (emphasis mine).
64. Ibid., 14.
65. James D. G. Dunn, "Altering the Default Setting: Re-envisaging the Early Transmission of the Jesus Tradition," *New Testament Studies* 49 (2003): 139-75.
66. Dunn, *Jesus Remembered*, 186.
67. Ibid., 175.
68. Ibid., 209. He goes on here to describe the fabric of a performance, "the oral transmission of Jesus tradition is a sequence of retellings, each starting from the same storehouse of communally

Dunn's insight into practice, would have to recognize that in the Gospels we do not get the historical Jesus but rather the remembered one. The continued identity-forming practices of storytelling and those practices initiated by the historical Jesus provide a structure of accountability within the community, but it's important to note that moving behind them is not possible.[69]

When the Gospels are seen as the dominant source of our knowledge as one that is contextually bound, it is hard to imagine them as sources for final objective historical accounts. The literary genre of Gospel is hardly compatible with the stance of an uncommitted historian. It is biased and intends to be persuasive because it is tied to the good news of Jesus who they inherently identify as the Christ. Not only that, but the popular distinction between the pre and post-Easter Jesus is not native to the authors who composed them nor the communities who cherished the Gospels, but more than that, it appears that there may be less light than expected when attempting to parse out those distinctions. The structure, selection, and shape of the narratives, sayings, deeds, mission, and passion of Jesus are uniquely tied to the Gospel-producing community's commitment to the resurrection of the cross-dead Jesus.[70] Unlike the other events attested to in the Gospels, the cross and resurrection of Jesus are inextricably tied to their meaning, purpose, and function as Gospels; in essence, they are part of the "canonic memory."[71] For the Gospels and their communities, it is hard to imagine the composition of the Gospels without the disciples of the crucified but resurrected Jesus.[72] It is important to point out here that we are only speaking of the embedded world of the disciples as

---

remembered events and teaching, and each weaving the common stock together in different patterns for different contexts."

69. Dunn makes an important distinction on the nature of historical reliability for the remembered Jesus, "This solution, applied to the Gospels, does not, of course, restore the old objectivity of the Gospels' meaning. But it does indicate a stronger possibility of recognizing a firmness to their perceived significance; it does prevent a failing apart into complete subjectivity and relativity; and from a Christian perspective in particular, it does attune with the more traditional thought of a trust-sustaining consensus within which matters of faith and conduct can be discussed and determined." Dunn, *Jesus Remembered,* 96.

70. Dunn's discussion of the nature of resurrection is helpful. Dunn, *Jesus Remembered,* 876-79.

71. Michael Welker, "Who is Jesus Christ for us Today?" *Harvard Theological Review* 95, no. 2 (Apr. 2002): 146. Welker is similar to Dunn in his assessment of the normative role of church practices for understanding the resurrection. See Michael Welker, "The Body of Christ, Holy Communion, and Canonic Memory," *Word & World* 22, no. 2 (Spring 2002): 164-69.

72. Francis Watson, "Is the Historian Competent to Speak of the Resurrection of Jesus? A Study in Hermeneutics," *Kerygma und Dogma* 55, no. 1 (2009): 52-72.

revealed in the Gospels. This does not necessitate any particular theological conclusion, a particular scientific explanation, nor a certain historical interpretation of the event. What is emphasized is essentially that, within the particular context of the Gospels, a claim about the reality of the resurrection is made and from the rest of the New Testament witness we can presume that they understood the resurrection to have made Jesus Christ a present and participatory reality for the Christian community.[73] While clear access to the real person behind the Gospel accounts is increasingly difficult to establish because of both the theological commitment of the sources and their function in the communities themselves, perhaps the scholarship is suggesting the historian's contribution is of a different sort. When the academic community is increasingly invested in the new conversations, political subversions, and hopeful protests present in the communities who birthed the Gospels, perhaps the best gain from our increasingly rich vision of first century Palestine are the witnesses in the Gospels themselves.

Christology From Within

How then does this new trajectory within Biblical studies open up new avenues for addressing the opening question, 'What did God do in Christ that we couldn't do for ourselves?' To those who have trouble answering the question because of methodological concerns, it offers a new starting point for Christology. It is not a new starting point, but an awareness of one already present through the Gospels. What is clear through this examination of New Testament studies is that the Gospels present Jesus Christ from and to the community of disciples. The texts themselves do not provide a means to get behind them to a Jesus who is not the central figure in the divine drama. On the other hand, despite being the clear operating assumption of the Gospels themselves, one cannot claim universality for the particular story being told on the evidence permitted by the texts alone. Here one can see the false dichotomy between a Christology from above and one from below. There is no secure below from which to start.

---

73. The Gospels themselves do not understand the resurrection to be an affirmation of the teachings of Jesus or a spiritual experience that inspires the continued presence of the Jesus movement. Because the resurrection is both a reality for the crucified Jesus and a hope for the disciple it seems appropriate to say that the New Testament would not permit a differentiation between the crucified Jesus and the risen Christ. The crucified Jesus may have been risen to more than he was, but the Christ of the New Testament is constitutively tied to the life of Jesus.

Likewise, the Gospels themselves make a network of Christological affirmations possible, one of which could be the Church's Creedal tradition, but the Creed itself was fashioned through debate with 'Biblical' heretics like Arius. The Gospels are unaware of starting Christology from above or below, and they exist as invitations to start life as a disciple from within. Christology is a disciple's dogma and as such, it starts from within the community seeking to celebrate, anticipate, and participate in the Good News of Jesus the Christ. The knowledge that is both gained and offered through the Gospels is not objective, but situated and participatory. On the other hand, the particular and local story of Jesus as presented in the Gospels has a universal horizon. This should raise questions about attempting to start the development of a Christology by bringing a closed anthropology or metaphysic in advance, something that regularly leads theologians to squeamish Christologies. Remembering Welker's discussion of a 'multi-systematic, polycontextual way of thinking,' we can instead see one's identity as a disciple as particularly situated and epistemologically open to bridge building between the different intellectual discourses about reality. In this way, one can be fully engaged in any truth- seeking conversation as a disciple, and in doing so be neither determined to fit Christ within a closed system nor uncover the entire universe in just one story because Christ is present along the way.

For the liberal theological tradition in particular, this new space being created by biblical scholarship is ripe for the theologian who wishes to articulate a liberal Christology more tightly connected to the living and diverse tradition of the church. Above, there was a discussion of the desire for the liberal theological tradition to emphasize the subjective nature of the Christian's faith commitment while affirming the legitimacy of reasoned reflection on history, sacred texts, and traditions. If a commitment to the historical endeavor does not reveal a giant chasm between the Jesus of history, for which there is little direct historical access, and the Christ of faith, the location of one's hermeneutical humility about the truth claims being asserted and the bulwark of theological revision needs to be moved. Instead, four diverse Gospel testimonies about the living presence of the once historical Jesus in the Christian community becomes the location for recognizing the tenuous nature of one's theological assertions. Not only does locating the Christological departure point of the theologian in this alternative framework recenter theologizing in the Gospels and their social matrix, but it does so while recognizing the transformative religious experience within the communities who created the Gospels. The historical endeavor cannot escape the influence of the communal and subjective structure of the early church. This does not prove the facticity of their accounts, but it undercuts the reductionistic tendencies of many past accounts of the historical Jesus. The theological conclusions that can be drawn from this starting point remain diverse and even progressive, yet they should not have the triumphalist *a priori* investments that only the reductionist Enlightenment-based line of thinking can give. Instead, the liberal tradition could find a freedom to both reclaim its sacred texts in new ways and develop a more robustly Christian testimony about Jesus the Christ, all while retaining the best of its legacy.

3

SPIRIT CHRISTOLOGY AND ITS RESURGENCE

Contemporary theology has seen a resurgence in Spirit Christologies. Drawing on some of the earliest New Testament traditions, theologians are now turning toward a Spirit Christology to address several most pressing Christological challenges. In this chapter, the Spirit Christologies of two different Catholic theologians, Roger Haight and Joseph Bracken, will be explored to show the contours, challenges, and promise of a Spirit Christology.

Before turning to Haight specifically, I should note the basic structure of a Spirit Christology and the shape of contemporary debates. A Spirit Christology, broadly speaking, develops the Biblical image of the Spirit, the ever-present and generative divine principle, such that the divinity of Jesus is understood as an emergent identity from a definitionally natural relationship God has with all humans. Different Spirit Christologies will articulate several variables within this picture differently, such as the role of sin, the nature of Jesus' faithfulness, or connections to Trinitarian relations. The key element, however, is that a Spirit Christology is a bibliocentric image that opens up a different trajectory of development from that of the more historically dominant *Logos* Christology.

It is not surprising that the attention of theologians has turned toward Spirit Christologies as of late. Three reasons dominate the turn. First, after coming face to face with the results from historical Jesus studies and the evolutionary trajectory of Christology in the early church, it is no longer credible to put the theological identification of Jesus as the eternal Son into the mouth of Jesus or even the confessions of all the New Testament authors and communities they represent. The diversity of Christological testimonies within the New Testament is hugely diverse and yet none of them include an explicitly Trinitarian account. Historically, the Trinity has been discovered exegetically when reading the texts through and with the Creedal hand of the tradition.[1] This means a Spirit Christology is both no longer required to be subservient to the *Logos* tradition and a way to let the robust language of the Spirit in the New Testament provide an alternative interpretive framework.

A second factor in the theological resurgence of Spirit Christologies is the challenge of religious Pluralism. The lived experience of a growing number of people within the church find any form of religious exclusivism problematic. When the particular figure of Jesus is understood in a way that limits access to God to this single point or relativizes the particularities of other traditions as functional only because of God's work in Christ, the good news of the one who died at the hands of imperial power seems to have inspired a missiology with the logic of Rome and not Galilee.[2] The theological response to pluralism that seeks to affirm the diversity of religious traditions by relativizing all of them is not as problematic to the culture as it is to theologians themselves. This tactic can take the form of a theory of religion, a call for mystical unity, or a proposal of an essential religion that gathers around some basic ethical principles. When every religious tradition is equally wrong and equally equipped to do whatever it is religions are intended to do, the challenge of religious pluralism is hardly handled. A Spirit Christology is attractive because it resists the exclusivist options by articulating the divinity of Jesus as a form of inspiration through the Spirit who is present to all, rather than a kind of divine invasion. For the pluralist, this same Spirit Christology opens up a way of affirming the unique

---

1. This does not mean that the church's conclusions established during the councils or elsewhere are not the proper account of Jesus' person. Anyone developing a Spirit Christology would have to allow the Spirit to play a role in the body of Christ and its reflection on the life of the one the Spirit uniquely animated. If the diversity of the Christologies in the New Testament tells us anything, it's that we can see a community of faith who is confident in their confession and the power of the presence of Christ, while the search for words and their meaning are open. This openness should, within a Spirit Christology, be a place we anticipate the activity and inspired multiplicity of the spirit-filled people. Is this not canonically insisted upon when the church canonized the four gospels? In doing so, they were drawing boundaries, including a conflicted diversity, resisting a harmonized telling, and doing so at the behest of the church's ears. When the canonized gospels are the ones that have life in the congregations of church across all its reach, any account of the Spirit which can facilitate a Spirit Christology could also advocate this type of logic when reading the movement of God in Christ's body.

2. These observations are not intended as an actual argument against the implied exclusivist or inclusivist proposals. Here I am simply wanting to highlight the conditions that created the context for a return to Spirit Christologies. As discussed in the introduction I am advocating a recognition of postmodern consciousness which includes pluralism, but not a specific answer.

and particular character of Jesus for the church, while also affirming the integrity and freedom of that same Spirit to do the same elsewhere. In this way, a Spirit Christology is for many contemporary theologians a way to preserve the particularity of Jesus and potentially affirm our neighbors' religious particularities.

The third factor in the resurgence of Spirit Christologies is its immediate applicability to Christian piety. To understand the person of Jesus by giving primary attention to his relationship to God through the Spirit opens up the doctrine of incarnation to the believer. Admonitions to take up the mind of Christ, to be the body of Christ, or receive the Spirit of Christ in a Spirit Christology all make the model of Jesus' own life more applicable to the disciple. The democratization of the divine embodying potential of the Spirit is attractive to many schools of theology. From Pentecostal theologians like Amos Yong, to social Trinitarians like Jürgen Moltmann, a Spirit Christology carries with it a model of Christian piety and practice. There is, however, a division among Spirit Christologies between those in which the Spirit is primarily understood in Trinitarian terms and those in which the Spirit is understood as the immanent principle of divine presence and activity. Both, however, easily produce accounts of Jesus with easily applicable models of piety.

A Postmodern Apologetic Christology

Roger Haight has contributed one of the most thorough proposals for a Spirit Christology in his book *Jesus: Symbol of God* and has continued to develop the argument in subsequent engagement afterward.[3] Haight intends his Christology to be a postmodern apologetic Christology that seeks to argue for a Spirit Christology over a *Logos* Christology. He does not, despite some of his critics, believe his proposal to be a deviation outside the Christian tradition. Understanding just what he sees as his theological proposal will provide some clarity.

By identifying his Christology as postmodern, he is not naming its methodology, but the cultural consciousness of its audience. Haight spends some significant time articulating just what characterizes "postmodern consciousness," bringing four primary features to the fore—cosmological

---

3. Roger Haight, *The Future of Christology* (New York: Continuum, 2007).

consciousness, social consciousness, historical consciousness, and pluralist consciousness.[4] These features are discussed above in the introduction, but for the purpose of engaging Haight's work, we should observe three things. First, he argues that these criticisms function in tandem with and often at the level of social assumptions to shape the collective consciousness of those he deems postmodern. Second, as part of his apologetic task, Haight does not make value judgements on any of these elements, but assumes them when beginning the constructive theological task. Third, these four elements individually make different religious truth claims culturally contested, but an element Haight does not emphasize is how false consciousness moves the point of contestation from the external affirmation to the one making the confession. Haight recognizes how postmodern consciousness cannot help but see the collective historical religious traditions as haunted by anthropological contributions. The challenge for Haight is thus recapitulating the tradition for a postmodern consciousness in a way that it is a net gain.[5]

As an apologetic postmodern Christology, Haight has a specific audience in mind; namely the doubters, skeptics, and post-church spiritual seekers in the West. He also characterizes this audience as those turned toward hints of transcendence amid secularity and pluralism.[6] In addressing these members on the edges and outskirts of the church, Haight recognizes just what is entailed in our cultural situation—Christology can no longer be determined and received based on authority alone.[7] In light of this, cultural given, he argues that Christology must begin from below, with the historical person of Jesus. Apart from being an aberration from the tradition, Haight describes the development of the tradition and its experiential groundings as originating from Jesus. The Christian is one in whom their experience of God and salvation is inseparably mediated by Jesus. This Jesus-mediated experience of God is "prior to and the

---

4. Roger Haight, *Jesus, Symbol of God* (Maryknoll, NY: Orbis Books, 2005), 330-34. See also Haight, *Dynamics of Theology*, (Maryknoll, NY: Orbis Books, 2001), 238-41.
5. Roger Haight, *Spiritual and Religious: Explorations for Seekers* (Maryknoll, NY: Orbis Books, 2016). This book, and in particular chapters two and eleven demonstrate just how compelling this proposal can be when turned from Christology to an invitation to Christian spirituality. The energy of the text oozes love, respect, and familiarity for a tradition in such a way that it is compelling and humble for its desired audience.
6. Haight, *Spiritual and Religious*, 24.
7. Haight, *Jesus, Symbol of God*, 29-30.

basis of the various interpretations of his identity and how salvation was won."[8] For Haight, it is the experience of God through Jesus which is the Christological norm, and not any articulation of it.[9] The fidelity of any account, and what holds the tradition together, is the history of this shared experience. From the New Testament until today, Christians have had their understanding of God and themselves definitively shaped and mediated by Jesus.[10] Methodologically, Haight's Spirit Christology is seen as the appropriate response for our time. When Christology is experientially centered, theologically correlational, and culturally postmodern, we require a Spirit Christology.

From Sacrament to Symbol

The apologetic nature of Haight's method is the primary reason he chose the concept of symbol for developing his Spirit Christology. As discussed below, the connections he draws between sacramental language and the symbolic are the essential structural elements of his Christology. Before developing his symbolic account of a Spirit Christology, his understanding of symbols needs to be noted.

Speaking definitionally, Haight says, "a symbol renders something else present and actual; a symbol is cognitive by making known something other than itself."[11] Haight gives six specific elements to symbolic communication.[12] While it is clear he is inheriting a philosophical conversation that runs through Rahner and Tillich, the way he construes the elements are nuanced for further Christological development. First, symbolic communication requires participation. For Haight, this includes a subjective, existential level to the communicative event. Despite the objective and reductive accounts of reality that dominate post-Enlightenment consciousness, Haight insists that any symbolic, religious, event necessarily draws the person into the question itself, for symbols seize the person. He makes this clear in his second element of a symbolic event by contrasting a symbol from a sign, emphasizing that unlike a

---

8. Roger Haight, "The Case for Spirit Christology," *Theological Studies* 53, no. 2 (1992): 264.

9. Roger Haight, "Logos Christology Today," in *From Logos to Christos: Essays on Christology in Honor of Joanne McWilliams*, ed. Ellen M. Leonard and Kate Merriman (Waterloo, Ont.: Wilfrid Laurier University Press, 2010), 105.

10. Haight, "The Case for Spirit Christology," 265.

11. Roger Haight, *Dynamics of Theology*, 130.

12. Haight, *Jesus, Symbol of God,* 196-202.

sign, a symbol mediates meaning by provoking the mind. A sign communicates referentially, but a symbol dialectically. A symbolic encounter requires engagement, reflection, and the tension that arises, necessarily, out of interpretation.

As Haight moves to the third element of a symbolic event, he narrows his scope to focus on the distinctively religious character, highlighting that religious symbols "participate in and point to transcendence."[13] Here, transcendence is used broadly to point to a structural relationship between all conditioned existence and that which is unconditioned. Whatever functions as a symbol is both necessarily part of conditioned existence and, in the event of a symbolically religious event, revelatory of something more. This more or transcendent element cannot be captured, determined, or fully grasped by the symbol itself. The meaning that comes from the event itself resists any face value assessment. For Haight, the reason is that religious symbolic events also reveal the essence of human existence. This fourth element, however, does not include an essentialized human essence that could function normatively across cultures, but includes an affirmation of a human aspiration, ideal, or self-knowledge that characterizes human engagement with the world.

The fifth element of a symbolic event is its multivalent structure. This means that symbols both reveal and conceal, while resisting any and every propositional account.[14] The presence of the transcendent in a symbolic event requires this resistance lest the symbol become an idol. The sixth and final element for Haight is the dialectical character of a symbolic event. Following Eliade, he argues that contrary things can be simultaneously asserted about a symbol because the symbol is not constitutively what is being symbolized.[15] This is the dialectic of all things sacred, between the holy and the worldly, the sacred and the profane, the contingent and the unconditioned. It is easy to see how this anticipates Christology. By describing a symbolic event as having both a multivalent structure and a dialectical character, the affirmation of both Jesus' humanity and his divinity is just a few steps away. A symbolic event requires a particular person, thing, or happening to occur, but when engaged symbolically,

---

13. Ibid., 200.
14. Haight, *Jesus, Symbol of God*, 201.
15. Mircea Eliade, *Images and Symbols: Studies in Religious Symbolism* (Princeton, NJ: Princeton University Press, 1991), 84-85. See also Haight, *Dynamics of Theology*, 132-35.

is seen as having genuinely more to show. The historical person of Jesus in his full humanity is then essential for Haight, but it is only when Jesus is seen as the Christ that God is mediated through him. The humanity of Jesus was not and could not be in jeopardy for him to have been also the Christ.

It is worth pausing here to anticipate what particular questions this rendering of a symbol could create. Given the ontological structure which supports this vision, we would identify the incarnation as symbolic. If the relationship of God and the world exemplified in each human being is structurally the same, the relationship between God the Father and the Son is potentially universal and its veracity is determined in part through the participation of the one who identifies Jesus as the Son. This ensures the full and innate humanity of Jesus, but makes his divinity an enacted feature for both Jesus and the believer. For Haight, this is not a concern but an asset that helps address his pluralistic question and apologetic concern. In fact, when interviewed about the specific role of his notion of symbol in his Christology, he stated, "If I had just titled the book *Jesus Sacrament of God* everything would have fallen into place in the Catholic world, no question asked."[16] The reason to avoid sacramental language for the symbolic was in part connected to his apologetic concern. Given the interdisciplinary conversations that can take place in discussions of symbolic events verses sacramental ones, Haight argues that the symbol is an avenue for communicating the gospel into disciplines closed off to God-talk. Even within postmodern consciousness, there is an opening to the transcendent at the level of the symbol. This communicative opening exists across academic disciplines often culturally hostile to God may have theological consequences, but Haight chose it for the apologetic task.

When Haight addresses concerns that the use of symbol is theologically reductionistic, he argues that a sacrament is a symbol used in a religious context. That is why his six elements above the religious nature of a symbolic event build from a more general notion of a symbol. As a finite thing, a symbol communicates something other than itself through its being itself, but it gets to something deeper than any finite thing can. Haight sees that there is a significant

---

16. Roger Haight, "A Postmodern Apologetic Christology with Roger Haight," interview by Tripp Fuller, September 21, 2015, in *Homebrewed Christianity,* podcast, MP3 audio, 17:40, https://homebrewedchristianity.com/2015/09/21/a-postmodern-apologetic-christology-with-roger-haight/.

realism to a symbol. A symbol not only communicates to one's consciousness but mediates another reality to that consciousness. A symbol does not point but mediates. In *Dynamics of Theology*, Haight gives the human body as an example of a concrete symbol of the inner self.[17] The human exterior is the expressive vehicle by which we communicate our inner-self. The only way one can know another is through a symbolic embodied expression mediated by a body. The body is the vehicle through which you can encounter the body of an other, not simply as a body, but as a self. The body is used to communicate through words, actions, signs, smiles, and more, but it is essential for Haight that the body must be understood symbolically to give full selfhood to the other. The body then is the primal symbol upon which human existence rests. Unlike some symbols that are notions, concepts, or happenings, the human body is the primal symbol upon which the others rest. In light of this robust affirmation of the symbol and the primal status of the body, Haight can begin a constructive proposal that Jesus as the symbol of God is not like all other religious symbols, but a more primal one that deserves a level of distinctiveness that sets Jesus apart for those who encounter him through faith as the Christ.[18] While this does not negate the recognition that the believer contributes to the symbolic encounter with Jesus as the Christ, it does so by acknowledging that any conscious participation in God "can only be existential, subjective, and experiential". And that the apologist can only "argue toward their truth, because faith is ultimately a function of freedom."[19] To state that Jesus is the symbol of God is, for Haight, a translation of the Chalcedonian definition. The perceived tension within his proposal is not identified with the creedal definition itself, but the dominating history of *Logos* Christology surrounding it. Haight argues that a Spirit Christology should replace this domination.

From *Logos* to Spirit

A Spirit Christology is not new in the history of the church, but rarely has it played the role of the dominant symbol for theological construction. However, Haight is not the first contemporary theologian to develop a Spirit Christology.

---

17. Haight, *Dynamics of Theology*, 137-39.
18. Haight, *The Future of Christology,* 46.
19. Haight, *Dynamics of Theology*, 141.

Paul Tillich, who likewise had a similar interest in religious symbols, developed his own Spirit Christology. Tillich describes a Spirit Christology as thus, "The divine Spirit was present in Jesus as the Christ without distortion. In him, the New Being appeared as the criterion of all Spiritual experiences in past and future. Though subject to individual and social conditions his human spirit was entirely grasped by the Spiritual Presence; his spirit was 'possessed' by the divine Spirit, or to use another figure, 'God was in him.' This makes him the Christ, the decisive embodiment of the New Being for historical mankind."[20] Tillich says that Jesus was "the bearer of the Spirit without limit"[21] and that the Spirit "created the Christ within Jesus."[22] For Tillich, the Spirit's creation of the Christ is both ultimately manifest decisively in Jesus, and likewise an event within the universal presence of the Spirit in creation.

Haight observes that the most common contemporary objections to a Christology from below are built on a fear that the conclusions will be reductionistic and unable to facilitate an account in which Jesus Christ is the object of one's faith.[23] He contests this by insisting that the first Christologies were in fact Christologies from below. In one sense, this is true in that the earliest disciples knew Jesus personally, but the earliest texts we have, both Paul's letters and the Gospels themselves, are post-Easter testimonies in which the identity of Jesus as the Christ is a conclusion to be witnessed to rather than a cumulative conclusion from below.[24] The thrust of Haight's critique of the tradition has been twofold, both in the dominance of *Logos* Christologies and the hypostatization of what was first a metaphor.[25] When taken together, the diversity of symbols and narratives of the New Testament that witness to God's

---

20. Paul Tillich, *Systematic Theology*, vol. 3 (Chicago: University of Chicago Press, 1976), 144.
21. Ibid., 145.
22. Ibid., 147.
23. Haight, "Logos Christology Today," 107.
24. A more charitable reading of the NT Christologies might be that the resurrection and continued presence of Jesus was the occasion for an eschatologically shaped hermeneutic of retrieval. Paul, who show little awareness and interest into the details of the historical Jesus' life, nonetheless insists that it was through the Spirit that Jesus was raised to the right hand of the Father. This conclusion he insisted meant we no longer see Jesus as some once did. This is not too far from the narrative of Peter in the NT who confesses the identity of Jesus as the Son of the living God correctly, only to misunderstand that this identity included the cross and eventually the inclusion of Gentiles.
25. Haight, "Logos Christology Today," 92.

presence in Christ are flattened and the trajectory of each line of thought is aligned with conclusions developed in the third and fourth centuries. Haight does not want to reject later conclusions, but argue that a Spirit Christology is a more adequate symbol among those present in scripture to organize our theological construction around given his apologetic intent for those that share a postmodern consciousness.[26]

The apologetic intent of Haight's work is a driving force throughout. His assumption is that the theological task is to give a credible account of the Christian faith, and given his audience, this becomes a task that must deal with their cognitive challenges. When given our historical consciousness, Haight's assessment is that a credible Christology for today must be from below. It is not simply the content of the quests for the historical Jesus that must be dealt with, but also the recognition that every age, culture, and people give historical and contextual account of themselves, meaning, and purpose.[27] If all truth is situated in its history, so were both Jesus and every person who has sought to confess him as the Christ throughout history. Thus, a two-fold Christology from below is necessary for Haight. First, for the humanity of Jesus to share fully in the conditions of our own humanity, he must be as historically conditioned as we are, finding his home in his first century context.[28] Second, like those who came before us, our own confession of Jesus as the Christ is a historical product. Not only is Jesus himself someone that needs to be understood from below, but the history of the church's confessions do as well.

For many, this may seem like a deflationary account of the Church's teachings, but for Haight, this misses the very heart of faith itself—namely that through it Jesus becomes the Christ, the very symbol of God. For the symbol of the faith to be a symbol, it must be living. And this life, while ever connected to the person of Jesus, is perpetually bringing confessions of faith to the disciples' tongues.[29] The dynamism inherent in his understanding of faith is something Haight believes should be part of any viable Christology.

---

26. Haight, "The Case for Spirit Christology," 259.
27. Haight, *Jesus, Symbol of God*, 332.
28. This does not mean that all one says theologically about Jesus is contained in his history, but namely that the presence of God in Christ does not abrogate or negate his historical situation. The symbolic structure of Haight's thought preserves the existential plausibility that Jesus' contemporaries that they could know Jesus not know him as the Christ.
29. Haight, "Logos Christology Today," 105.

Christologies, Haight describes, "are formulations that express, or explain, or identify who Jesus is based on the experience of faith that Jesus bears God's salvation."[30] In examining his Spirit Christology, one must look at both the role of the Spirit between Jesus and God, along with the role of the Spirit in the ongoing life of the church. Said another way, a symbolic Spirit Christology must give an account of both the person of Jesus' relationship to God and how it occasioned salvation for others and the relationship of the disciple to God as mediated by Jesus.[31] Between considering the historical Jesus and the situated experience and testimonies of the Christian community, the connective tissue for Haight's proposal is his genetic approach that sketched the origins, proposals, and development of Christology. A Spirit Christology is such that its account of God as Spirit can correlate with what we can reconstruct of Jesus' own life, as well as the diversity and developing articulation of the church and the experience of faith that gives credulity to the skeptical believer. For Haight, this means that there are three important criteria to a satisfactory Christology.[32] First, it must display fidelity to the foundational testimony of Jesus as the Christ in the New Testament and secondarily the continued testimony in the Creeds and tradition. A Spirit Christology emphasizing the presence of God as Spirit always already in the world resists understanding the incarnation as an aberration but posits it as a fruit of this relationship. The Spirit of God that was present before Jesus in his ministry, reshaped through Easter, and present in the life of the church, must remain faithful to the life of the Spirit. As Christians, the reference point must remain Christ. For Haight, it is through Jesus that we are to read the Creeds and not vice versa. Haight's second criterion for an adequate Christology is intelligibility. By intelligibility, Haight refers not simply to his apologetic audience, but also to the significance of the claim itself. A non-intelligible account of Christ requires an act of faith from the believer that is more akin to intellectual assent against reason rather than a crafted testimony to a way of being in the world—namely the lived reality of those whose experience of God is mediated by Jesus. Because of Haight's experiential emphasis, this notion of intelligibility is less like a logical syllogism and more

---

30. Haight, "The Case for Spirit Christology," 280.
31. Haight, *Jesus, Symbol of God*, 447.
32. Haight, *The Future of Christology*, 44-45.

like a moving love poem. Haight's third criterion is empowerment. A Christology done well must empower faithful Christian living. Christology is a disciple's discipline and cannot ultimately be separated from the call of Christ to the community of disciples. All three criteria lead Haight toward a Spirit Christology.

Structuring a Spirit Christology from Below

Before outlining the structure of Haight's Spirit Christology, it is helpful to note just how he understands the Spirit as an image present in the Biblical tradition that Jesus and the disciples who witnessed to his identity inherited. The soundscape of the symbol of the Spirit of God is primarily the Hebrew scriptures. For Haight, the Biblical symbol of the Spirit is both definitely God and a referent to God from a particular vantage point—namely the Spirit refers to God "at work, as active, and as power, energy, or force that accomplishes something."[33] We see the Spirit of God in scripture as God present, personal, and participating in the world. It is this immanent principle of divine activity that is not *a priori* understood as a person within the trinity. The Spirit is not a direct referent to God as God is in Godself, but as God who has been revealed through divine engagement in the world. "The Spirit is experienced; the Spirit is grace; the Spirit is salvation. The effects of the Spirit in the community and the individual lives of its members can be named: they are faith, love, forgiveness, redemption, justification, sanctification, adoption by God, reconciliation, freedom from sin, illumination, liberation, empowerment, and charismatic gifts of service to the community."[34] If we understand the Spirit of God to be God engaged and invested in the world, it should not be shocking that one could use it to develop a Christology.

Haight defines Spirit Christology as "one that 'explains' how God is present and active in Jesus, and thus Jesus' divinity, by using the biblical symbol of God as Spirit, and not the symbol *Logos*."[35] Haight develops three distinct stages of the Spirit as the image becomes used to articulate the person of Jesus. While it begins with the Hebrew scriptures and comes to fruition in

---

33. Haight, *Jesus, Symbol of God,* 448.

34. Haight, "The Case for Spirit Christology," 270.

35. Ibid., 257.

the early church's post-Easter confessions, Haight dwells on the fact that the image of the Spirit was part of Jesus' own self-understanding. He notes that Jesus taught that the Spirit was central to the life and ministry of a disciple, and that the Spirit served as an image of continuity between the disciples' connection to Jesus before and after Easter in both Paul and the Synoptics.

The structure then for a Spirit Christology from below begins with Jesus. Haight recognizes that we have scant secure historical data to work with, given the oldest texts we have are overwhelmingly Christian, but surely these texts have as their referent the historical person of Jesus. The person of Jesus, the disciples' experience of him, and their earliest theological accounts are foundational. In these, the historical person of Jesus remains the concrete historical symbol of God, thus making his life, ministry, and teachings determinative for Christology.[36] The second element structuring a Spirit Christology from below is the Easter experience. Haight argues that the intensity of the debate about the nature of the historical resurrection has distracted many from its existential focus. Summarizing his affirmation, Haight states that, "the resurrection was the exaltation and glorification of the whole individual person called Jesus of Nazareth. The one who was resurrected is no one else than Jesus, so that there is continuity and personal identity between Jesus during his lifetime and his being with God."[37] By distinguishing the Disciples' Easter experience and God's resurrecting of Jesus, Haight does two important things. First, he draws a continuity between the first disciples' experience of the risen Christ and our own.[38] Second, Haight insists upon "Jesus being risen" as the moment that Christology emerges, for it is here where "the connecting link between Jesus in his ministry and the emergent Christian faith" is forged.[39] The normative confession for Haight is that Jesus was the subject of the resurrection and that it was through this event that the disciples converted from their disillusionment after the cross to a robust faith.[40] Out of

---

36. Haight, *The Future of Christology*, 44.

37. Haight, *Jesus, Symbol of God*, 124.

38. Here Haight uses the Emmaus story in Luke as a model for explaining the resurrection. There he highlights a four-point theory in which 1) a strong memory of Jesus, 2) a strong hope and faith, 3) an event of grace or revelation, and 4) the narration and witnessing to this Easter hope through the empty tomb and appearance narratives. Haight, *Jesus, Symbol of God*, 136-39.

39. Haight, *The Future of Christology*, 203 (emphasis in original).

40. Ibid., 45.

a disciples' Easter experience, both then and today, comes the third element that structures a Spirit Christology—namely the interpretations of Jesus as Christ by his followers. As James Dunn stated in his detailed analysis of New Testament Christologies, "there is no single coherent understanding or presentation of Christ which meets us after Easter."[41] For this reason alone, Haight has deep concerns about the domination of the *Logos* over time. He argues that when the concept of the *Logos* reigns, the other images become subservient to this single image, which problematizes itself. To discern elements of unity amidst the polyphony of witnesses, Haight observes that they all originate from an experience—the experience of Jesus as "the bearer of God and God's salvation."[42] Haight also observes that the fact that Jesus is the mediator of God's salvation runs throughout the testimonies in the New Testament, which justifies the soteriological situation in which his person is understood.

If Christology emerged because Jesus Christ mediated the presence and salvation of God, Haight argues that it must be the same experiential emergence today. This is the place where his understanding of the Spirit and symbol meet, for the Biblical image of the Spirit provides the organizational center for an account of Jesus that recognizes his concrete symbolic mediation of God. In the ministry of Jesus, it was the reign of God that dominated his teachings, parables, and agenda. Through all his wondrous acts of healing, embrace, and challenge, it was the reign of God that was being enacted. For Haight, it is the New Testament's emphasis on the Spirit's role in all of this that is essential for grasping the character of Jesus' person and ministry, for through it all the reign of God was not offered as a prediction, but as a call to participation.[43] Haight states, "By being a symbol of God, by mediating an encounter with God, Jesus reveals God as already present and active in human existence. Historically, he does this both by being and by making God present thematically through his words, actions, and whole person. Jesus reveals by causing in the persons who come to him in faith an analogous reflective awareness of the presence of God

---

41. James D. G. Dunn, *Unity and Diversity in the New Testament: An Inquiry into the Character of Earliest Christianity* (London: SCM, 2006), 216.
42. Haight, *The Future of Christology*, 45.
43. Haight, *Jesus, Symbol of God*, 97-99, 108.

to them."[44] Jesus' own radical fidelity to God and God's reign was not exclusive, for Jesus called his disciples to practice it and share it to the ends of the earth. Jesus' life in the Spirit was not a life he alone experienced, but through the Spirit, the disciples also came to share in it. Jesus' own spirit-filled living became the situation of revelation for the disciples. In this way, Haight's understanding of Jesus is not distinct from the disciples because of the quantitative separation between his fidelity to God and theirs. While this may be true, a Spirit Christology is not simply an articulation of how the Spirit inspired Jesus' life in a unique and particular way; it is also about how God as Spirit was mediated to those who came to faith in Jesus as the Christ. This is where Haight argues for the qualitative distinctiveness of Jesus' person. For the disciple, their relationship to God is not the result of some teaching or wisdom gained from Jesus, a wisdom that could have possibly come from elsewhere and whose vitality can easily be separated from Jesus of Nazareth. This Spirit Christology centers on Jesus, the concrete symbol of God and cannot retain its life apart from him and this is intrinsic to Haight's symbolic account of the Spirit. "The symbol of the Spirit more forthrightly makes the claim that God, God's very self, acted in and through this Jesus."[45] For Haight, nothing less than God was at work in Jesus and we do not need yet the trajectory of the *Logos* to make this affirmation.

Beyond meeting his criteria for an adequate Christology, in final comparison with the *Logos* tradition, Haight emphasizes that the metaphor of the Spirit does not have a history of hypostatization. By personifying God's revealing power as the *Logos* and then applying it to Jesus, the church ends up giving this metaphor a metaphysical compliment that Haight finds problematic.[46] Haight sees a certain problem inherent in much of the Christological debate about *Logos* and Spirit Christologies, namely that there are many defenders of *Logos* Christology who try to move beyond the predicament of hypostatization by positing the possibility of or even affirming multiple incarnations. Haight's issue is not the desire to affirm the reality of God's revelatory presence in other people or other traditions or even to insist

---

44. Ibid., 359.
45. Haight, "The Case for Spirit Christology," 272.
46. Haight, "Logos Christology Today," 94.

that in preserving God's own freedom one cannot close off such a possibility. Haight insists that the character of a *Logos* Christology has undergone a significant symbolic shift when multiple incarnations are deemed as even a possibility.[47] When the singularity, finality, exclusivity, and qualitatively distinct accounts of divinity are altered, the difference between a Spirit and *Logos* Christology is minimal. The concerns being addressed by this symbolic reworking of the concept of the *Logos* are much more natural to a Spirit Christology.

Symbolic Work and the Life of God

With the basic structure of Jesus the symbol of God, an understanding of the work of Jesus follows that emphasizes Jesus' role as representative. Haight here points toward the influence of Sollee, arguing that Jesus functions as a representative in two ways.[48] Jesus symbolizes God for us and Jesus is God's symbol communicating to us. Said another way, Jesus is God's representative of humanity before God and God's revelation to us. This sets up an Irenaean account of the atonement, following his developmental worldview and pedagogical account of the narrative of salvation.[49] In Irenaeus' account, the story of Jesus then required more than a single transactional event to set things to right with God because the whole of humanity needed to be saved and recapitulated in the life of Jesus.[50] This means the entire life of Jesus, its stages, trials, experiences, death, and innocent human suffering, are all part of the process of redemption.[51] Thus, in being saved from sin, we are not being saved simply from God's wrath, history, matter, or the world, but saved into the divine life of the Spirit which death will not conquer.[52] By innocently going to his cross, Jesus takes on to himself the atoning act of representing to the Father the

47. Ibid., 95.
48. Dorothee Sölle and Luise Schottroff, *Jesus of Nazareth* (Louisville, KY: Westminster John Knox, 2002).
49. Haight, *Jesus, Symbol of God*, 217-18.
50. Haight, *The Future of Christology*, 100-101.
51. Jaroslav Pelikan, *The Emergence of the Catholic Tradition (100-600)*, The Christian Tradition: A History of the Development of Doctrine, vol. 1 (Chicago: University of Chicago Press, 1971), 144.
52. Haight, *Jesus, Symbol of God*, 219.

full reality of human existence.[53] Here the cross becomes paradigmatic of the suffering caused by sin and evil throughout history. Connecting this Irenaean view to the theological challenges of both the problem of evil and the struggle for liberation to the essence and existence of God, Jesus makes a symbolic atonement by representing them through taking on. Important to note here is that for Haight it is only through the resurrection that this negative experience gains its symbolic importance. It is not then the innocent and tortured death of Jesus that saves, but God and God alone.[54] Through God's resurrection of the crucified one, the promise of God for all humanity is revealed—especially those who met a violent and unjust end.

Haight's development of a revelatory theory of atonement is an important part of his apologetic task. For many in his stated audience, the popular understanding of the atonement is riddled with an Anselmian logic that trivializes the life of Jesus, assumes a three-stage Christology, and understands the suffering of Jesus within a penitential framework. When it comes to salvation, Haight rejects assigning any positive value to the actual suffering of Jesus.[55] The cross may be revelatory of sin and evil, but not necessary for divine victory. The death of Jesus is then the tragic situation to which the resurrection comes. Haight understands that it was through the resurrection that God's power to save is revealed, even when faced with radical evil. The symbolic word of the cross is not something that can be isolated from either the ministry of Jesus in which the nature, presence, and passion of God was revealed, nor from the resurrection in which Jesus' own commitment to the reign of God is validated and God's power to save revealed. As Haight puts it, it is the "Spirit (that) impels Jesus' fidelity to his vocation, even to the end" and that it is God who saves by "raising him from death," making Jesus truly the "new Adam, the pioneer, and the first-born of many."[56] This means that a Spirit Christology includes an "uncentering of the resurrection in Christian faith," but not to relegate its importance, but to let the content of its power be determined

---

53.   Haight draws a connection here between himself and Schillebeeckx, who said, "In Jesus, both God's trust in man and man's response of trust in God take on their definitive historical form." Edward Schillebeeckx, *Interim Report on the Books Jesus and Christ*, (New York: Crossroad, 1981), 109.
54.   Haight, *The Future of Christology*, 102.
55.   Ibid.
56.   Ibid.

lly by the Spirit-filled ministry of Jesus.[57] Following Jon Sobrino, ecognizes that the logic of resurrection faith has historically been to the cross and ministry of Jesus, which in turn leads to the continued oppression of many.[58] The Spirit of God which animated the ministry of Jesus was for these very people ignored by much of the church. If it was indeed the Spirit which anointed Jesus to preach good news to poor, liberation for the captives, and proclaim the year of the Lord's favor, and it was this Spirit which sustained both the faith of Jesus and the disciples' faith in Jesus, no account of God's work in Christ can relegate the actual mission of the Spirit. For Haight, a Spirit Christology insists that humans are not meant to endure suffering and injustice, but rather engage, resist, and work to overcome it, for God as Spirit is empowering this very type of work.[59] The necessary accompanying statement is thus that through the cross, the absolute mystery of God came to encounter the full negativity of human existence and yet even this death did not have the final word. In the resurrection, "only God and the resurrected life that God promises are ultimate."[60]

For the Christian believer, one's relationship with God as mediated by Jesus is here distinctively Christian. Because religious pluralism is both a central concern for Haight's work and a necessary conundrum for a theologian seeking to address postmodern consciousness, just how this Spirit Christology from below can respond is quite important. The primary concern for Haight is the assumption that religions are inherently competitive. He wants to argue for and develop a noncompetitive vision for religious pluralism that comes out of his Christology, demonstrating that this noncompetitive position actually coheres with the tradition, rather than parting ways with it. What is important for Haight then is an affirmation of the absoluteness of Jesus as God's medium of salvation and not, as the Church has often assumed, its exclusiveness. Jesus the symbol of God can be affirmed as decisive, definitive, and final for Christians. However, the means to make this affirmation is existential. The "existential relationship of the believer to Jesus" makes this distinctive

---

57.   Haight, *Jesus, Symbol of God, 149-50.*
58.   Ibid., 148.
59.   Haight, *Spiritual and Religious*, 56.
60.   Ibid., 56.

experience of God possible.[61] Because of his symbolic account of religious experience and his foundational reworking of Christology in his Spirit account, it is easy to see the ability to have non-competitive relations with other faith traditions. As Haight sees it, the challenge is describing how his vision is still both trinitarian and pluralistic. The existential character of the believer's response is his starting place. He notes that to confess Jesus as the Christ is to give testimony to an experience that is trinitarian in nature. For Haight, "theology begins with the experience itself," which is for the Christian, first Christological.[62] This means that one cannot begin Christian theology with the Trinity. It is Christological proposals, which are normative for accounts of the Trinity. Within a Spirit Christology, two emphases are important. The first is the recognition that it was the Spirit, which inspired both the person of Jesus and the believer who receives Jesus Christ in faith. The very dynamism of the disciples' faith as depicted in the Gospels and much of Paul's imagery of life in the early church are described in relation to the Spirit. Haight's second emphasis is a consequence of his symbolic account of Christ, namely that every experience of Jesus as the Christ is always an experience of both Jesus and the Spirit. Apart from the work of the Spirit, the person of Jesus simply cannot be received in faith.

These two emphases set up an account of the Trinity from below. Because Trinitarian theology is both historically and logically dependent on Christology, to understand the Trinity truly, one must begin there.[63] Seen in this perspective, the doctrine of the Trinity is less an account of God as God is in Godself, but as one that originates from the experience of God as the one who saves through Jesus Christ. The Trinity may be secondary to the experience of salvation, but to give a Christian account of salvation, we need the Trinity. For Haight, the Trinity is the shorthand referent to the larger narrative of salvation. This story of salvation, he argues, "cannot be told without reference to God creator, Jesus Christ savior, and God as Spirit at work in the church and in the world," which means, "an account of Christian salvation is unimaginable without trinitarian language."[64] If the experience of salvation is the point of Trinitarian language,

---

61. Haight, "The Case for Spirit Christology," 282.
62. Haight, *The Future of Christology, 53.*
63. Haight, *Jesus, Symbol of God,* 480ff.
64. Haight, *The Future of Christology, 53.*

it should be understood as salvation language. For those who have encountered God as mediated by Jesus, Trinitarian language is fitting and proper precisely because of this encounter. This means that for Haight, the Trinity is primarily understood in economic terms. The popular method of those after Rahner to draw a revelational connection between the economic and immanent Trinity need to recognize the speculative character and experiential grounds for the Trinity. In protecting the absolute mystery of God's Being, Haight also gives priority to the activity of the Spirit who was present and presents Christ to the believer.

The World and Triune Activity

Joseph Bracken is a Jesuit philosophical theologian who is a committed neo-Whiteheadian. Over the course of his career, he has spent a great deal of time working in the fields of religion and science, while developing his own elaborate doctrine of God. Later in his career, he turned to the more confessionally centered doctrines such as the Trinity and his own proposal for a Spirit Christology. By beginning with Bracken's Open and Relational account of the Trinity and seeing its utilization in constructing a Spirit Christology, several features will enhance or contrast with Haight's. And after sketching out Bracken's thought, a more deliberate comparison will be made. Anticipating the mutual stretching between both Haight's and Bracken's positions, it should be noted at the outset that while they are both developing Spirit Christologies, Haight begins from below and Bracken with the trinity. Haight gives a thoroughgoing existential account of the Christ and Bracken a metaphysical depiction. Despite these differences of trajectory, they both move toward the other's starting point. Here we turn to Bracken's understanding of the trinity.

Bracken has developed one of the most comprehensive accounts of the trinity from a process perspective. As a Jesuit, his journey to process thought led him through graduate studies in Thomism and German Idealism before discovering Whitehead. Both his intellectual pedigree and personal commitment to the faith makes his proposal rich and unique. Bracken is committed to developing a comprehensive neo-Whiteheadian worldview that is thoroughly Trinitarian. His desire to engage not only in theological dialogue, but also in philosophical, scientific, and interdisciplinary endeavors shaped his methodology. On what terms could a trinitarian worldview engage in interdisciplinary talk? Philosophically. Therefore, Bracken begins his trinitarian investigation by examining what larger philosophical predicament is being explored within theological constructions of the Trinity. He thus first identifies the problem of the one and the many.[65] In fact, Bracken suggests that this problem is not only one that shapes most of the West's philosophy but also the different accounts of the trinity. When a philosophical theologian is asked to explain how God can be three persons with one divine essence, they are hearing the problem of the one and the many. Bracken develops a theological account of this confessional piece of theology by appropriating his version of process philosophy.[66] First, Bracken wants to describe the shared divine essence, also referred to as the one, as the infinite field of activity.[67] This field of activity is developed by a modification of Whitehead's concept of 'society.' For Whitehead, a society is as close as he gets to articulating the endurance of identity from one event of becoming to another.[68] Bracken takes the concept from *Process and Reality* and develops it such that a society both structures the layers of relational complexity within a moment of becoming like that of a body's respiratory system over the organs which make it up, and preserves the dynamism of the relationship from moment to moment. A field of activity can then endure while always being a set of actual entities. If the shared divine essence of the Trinity is a field of activity, the three persons should find their unity within it.[69] Bracken notes that within the classical tradition, there was an assertion that the three persons are different and distinct only because of their relations. For example, the Father is not the Son, and the Son is not the Father. That is a definitional distinction. Likewise, one is not a Father

---

65. Joseph A. Bracken, *The World in the Trinity: Open-Ended Systems in Science and Religion* (Minneapolis, MN: Fortress, 2014), 76.

66. Ibid., 66.

67. Joseph A. Bracken, *Subjectivity, Objectivity, & Intersubjectivity: A New Paradigm for Religion and Science* (West Conshohocken, PA: Templeton Foundation, 2009), 133-37. Later Bracken changes his preferred articulation to "system" over "structured field of activity" after engaging systems theory in the sciences. Because the majority of his work on Christology employs the term "field of activity" more, I have continued to use it in this composition. See Bracken, *The World in the Trinity*, 110-12.

68. Alfred North Whitehead, *Process and Reality*, 34-35, 100-105. See also Bracken's modification of the Whiteheadian society. Joseph A. Bracken, *God: Three Who Are One* (Collegeville, MN: Liturgical, 2008), 114.

69. Joseph A. Bracken, "Panentheism and the Classical God-World Relationship: A Systems-Oriented Approach," *American Journal of Theology & Philosophy* 36, no. 3 (September 2015): 224-25.

without a Son and no Son can be a Son without a Father. The difference here between these two persons is determined by their relationship to one another. Nothing external to the relations of the three persons shapes their relations, and nothing external then can possess or determine their shared field of activity. In their relations to one another, these three persons co-constitute an enduring field of activity, namely the divine essence, which he terms the divine matrix.[70] This means that the divine essence can be shared equally, for the origin of the field is not the Father (the one) but the relations of the three.

Just because Bracken develops an understanding of the Trinity by appropriating his neo-Whiteheadian philosophy does not mean he has succeeded. As a philosopher, Whitehead had more than one ultimate.[71] God was not alone in God's divine eternity and then began to create the world, for God's creative activity was not a solo affair. In each moment of becoming, God, Creativity, the World, and the Forms were all participants.[72] The West and even other process thinkers have found ways of locating the Forms within the mind of God, but Bracken must now articulate a doctrine of creation out of nothing and somehow give an account of creativity that coheres with his understanding of the trinity. When dealing with creativity, he echoes John Cobb's distinction of God as the Ultimate Actuality and creativity as Ultimate Reality by distinguishing between The Entity and The Non-Entity.[73] Creativity as the Non-Entity is developed out of an engagement with Schelling in which there is an abyss, an underground, from which all actuality comes. This depth is of God but not God, for God is an actual entity and creativity is non-actual. Beyond God's relationship to creativity is the problematic assertion for the Christian tradition that God and the world are co-eternal. Bracken does not take up the mantle of other process theologians and protest creation out of nothing as a doctrinal occupation of the tradition.[74] Instead, he argues that the life of the Trinity in the divine field of activity is such that it desires to share life freely and not out of necessity. The divine matrix is the space in which creation

---

70. Joseph A. Bracken, *The Divine Matrix: Creativity as Link between East and West* (Eugene, OR: Wipf & Stock, 2006).

71. Whitehead, *Process and Reality*, 7, 20-21.

72. Ibid., 20-21.

73. John B. Cobb Jr., "Ultimate Reality: A Christian View," *Buddhist-Christian Studies* 8 (1988): 50-64.

74. See Catherine Keller, *The Face of the Deep: A Theology of Becoming* (London: Routledge, 2003) and David Ray Griffin, *Evil Revisited: Responses and Reconsiderations* (Albany, NY: State University of New York Press, 1991).

comes into being. The infinite field of activity creates space for a large collection of finite fields of activity. Creation has space and freedom to be itself in relation to others and to God. Bracken pushes back against the common process analogy of soul-body for God-World.[75] He rejects the mutual dependence of the image, but not just for God. Yes, God chose to create out of the over-flowing love within the divine matrix, but when God created God did not create a body part but rather a genuine other. This other finds its origin within the divine matrix but is not determined by it. When there is a free correspondence, or a mutual in-dwelling, between the divine field of activity and a given finite field, you can see Bracken's understanding of the kingdom of God. As he puts it, "I picture the kingdom of God as the space or field of activity co-created by the three divine persons and all their creatures since the beginning of time...it is a network of relationships that have stood the test of time and that in retrospect have given meaning and value not simply to human history but to the whole course of cosmic evolution from the moment of the Big Bang onward."[76]

Bracken shares Haight's concern about religious pluralism in light of the specificity of the Christian confession of God as Triune. By developing a trinitarian model of the one and the many and then abstracting the philosophical model out of its confessional context, Bracken turns to the diversity of religious expressions. Following Mark Heim, yet also implied in his system itself, he creates a threefold series of religious categories: those in which God is seen as one, God as three, and then those non-theistic religious visions beyond God. He notes the correspondence of these categories to the divine essence, the divine matrix, and creativity respectively, but he sees that the trinitarian lessons are more fruitful for relations themselves. For example, just as the divine persons need each other, so too the religions need each other. As the divine persons are defined by their differences and yet this enables their unity, so too the religions should cherish their mutual distinctiveness while seeking unity. Thus, just as the divine matrix is enlivened by its relations, so too the religions should seek to be enlivened and learn from one another.[77]

---

75. Bracken, *God: Three Who Are One*, 79.
76. Joseph A. Bracken, *Christianity and Process Thought: Spirituality for a Changing World* (Philadelphia: Templeton Foundation, 2006), 55.
77. Bracken, *The Divine Matrix*, 137-38.

Trinitarian Spirit Christology

One of the major points of contrast between Bracken and Haight is the role of the Trinity. For Bracken, it is the new metaphysical account of the Triune God that establishes the framework for his Spirit Christology, making his version definitionally triune. The key philosophical concepts that he brings into his Christological proposal are a metaphysics based on intersubjective relations and the possibility for simultaneous mutual causality. While framed in his account of the Trinity, Bracken sees that they function as valid philosophical constructions on their own.[78] Bracken's Spirit Christology is, like the Trinity before it, a doctrine in which the problem of the one and the many is at play; namely, the question is, how are there two complete and distinct natures in one person? Appropriating the concepts developed in his account of the Trinity, he describes the two natures as two fields of activity.[79] Since fields of activity can overlap and interpenetrate each other without compromising the integrity of either, both a human and divine field is not problematic. More so, given Bracken's account of the divine matrix and its decision to create the space necessary for creation within the divine matrix itself, there is already a possibility for mutual indwelling. Bracken identifies events of correspondence when a finite field of activity corresponds to that of the divine matrix as the kingdom of God, the 'already' of the coming consummation of God in which creation comes to participate fully in the divine life.[80] Events of correspondence are natural in that they are the fulfillment of creation's telos, and yet they are intermittent. How in the one person of Jesus do these two natures continuously cooperate? Bracken's answer is the Spirit.

Bracken is different here from many Spirit Christologies, which are often adoptionist or Arian, for Bracken argues that at the moment of incarnation when the Son became flesh, the Spirit anointed Jesus as both Son of God and as a human field of activity.[81] The Spirit, following Augustine, is the love which binds the Father and the Son. This results in a single person who shared

---

78. Bracken, *Subjectivity, Objectivity*, 136-37.
79. Joseph A. Bracken, "Trinitarian Spirit Christology: In Need of a New Metaphysics?" *Theological Studies* 72, no. 4 (2011): 757.
80. Bracken, *Christianity and Process Thought*, 55-59.
81. Bracken, "Trinitarian Spirit Christology," 757.

completely in two natures. As Bracken puts it, "there was an ongoing reciprocal causality between the divine and the human in Jesus' experience… consciously or unconsciously he was always responsive to the will of the Father in heaven even as he retained the freedom to respond to the Father his own way."[82] One may question Bracken's account because the Gospels themselves lack much evidence that the Spirit's presence in Jesus' life was such that he shared the life of the divine matrix. Here, however, one sees that his trinitarian vision and philosophical solutions are given interpretive priority. He argues that one must first rightly understand the definition of a person, which he connects to his concept of a society.[83] A person is the higher order subjectivity that functions with a mind and will within a field of activity. For example, in the human it is not one's organs that possess a personality, fall in love, and create art. They are necessary for the existence of the mind but do not determine it. Likewise, through the Spirit it is not the subjectivity of Jesus that is the higher order, but that of the Son within the divine matrix.[84] Bracken argues that the nature of the overlapping fields of activity within Jesus that were secured by the Spirit from the moment of incarnation are both preserved with complete integrity although it is Jesus' identity as the Son that functions as the higher order subjectivity.

When Bracken turns to scripture to locate the operations of his Spirit Christology, not unlike his doctrine of the Trinity, he explains that it is implicit and not explicit. For example, in calling God *Abba*, Jesus displayed an intimacy with the divine that he even invited others into, as he prioritized parental images of God in Hebrew scriptures over legal and royal ones. Regularly Bracken focuses on the Johannine Jesus' teaching on the Spirit to understand both the relationship of the Son to the Father and the disciples' participation in God. For Bracken, this intimacy is historical evidence of the divine communitarian life that Jesus shared in the divine matrix as preserved through the Spirit.[85] The divine matrix could be present and active in the one person of Jesus without conscious recognition of it. After his exaltation 'to the right hand of the Father'

---

82. Bracken, *The World in the Trinity*, 130.
83. Bracken, "Trinitarian Spirit Christology," 758-59.
84. Bracken, *The World in the Trinity*, 129-31.
85. Ibid., 133.

as the tradition describes it, Jesus would come to know what was always already the case—that his one person fully shared in two natures.

It is here that we touch on something worth pausing over. First, Bracken can describe something within his neo-Whiteheadian scheme that renders the traditional affirmations of the incarnation and Trinity more explicable. This is an impressive feat. For those invested in reappropriating the tradition, his Spirit Christology can avoid falling into an Arian or adoptionistic mode. Perhaps what is most problematic is his account of personhood. If the person is the higher order subjectivity present in a field of activity, in what way is the person of Jesus truly human as the rest of humanity experiences its own subjectivity? Bracken, who follows the German Idealists in advocating for a single incarnation, implies that no one else other than Jesus has a subjectivity higher than their human subjectivity that is constitutively operating above, through, and with it. Bracken argues that given the nature of simultaneous mutual causation in an intersubjective context, the divine subjectivity within Jesus functions as a persuasive form of empowerment for his human consciousness.[86] Should another human field of activity practice the same empowered fidelity of Jesus, it would constitute the 'already' of the kingdom of God made present, and this moment in which the two natures/fields of activity shared in a full mutuality would come into being and go out.

In Bracken's Spirit Christology, the mutuality has neither a coming into nor going out of Jesus. He simply takes it for granted that Jesus' divine status was a settled given throughout his life. The mutuality was not an act of the human person's mind or will, but given to it from the incarnation and then secured throughout by the Spirit. What is described in the Gospels as the radical faithfulness of Jesus is true, but only up to a point. If the exhalation of Jesus reveals that the higher order subjectivity operating in his person was the eternal Son and that the Spirit secured this bond, his faithfulness is unlike the faithfulness of his disciples in kind and not degree. Thus, the presence of the kingdom of God he brought was unlike those who came after, for no one else has yet been possessed by the Spirit in the same manner. In fact, when Bracken goes on state, "the historical Jesus and the cosmic Christ refer to one and the same individual entity who is both human and divine at the same time," he wants

---

86. Ibid., 133.

to resist Gordon Kaufman's relativizing "wider view" of the Christ.[87] We can affirm the particularity of Jesus without needing to incorporate the subjectivity of the human Jesus into the higher subjectivity of the Son throughout the entirety of his life. A form of emergent adoptionist Christology seems just as appropriate, if not more so, for an evolutionary panentheist. The faith-fullness of the Spirit-filled Jesus could be understood as the very grounds for which the union of the Father to Son in the Spirit was born. The emergence of a qualitatively different relationship with God—a God who too is being changed by God's own participation and self-investment in history—would not necessarily negate its particularity or even its finality. Given Bracken's own description of the multifaceted and continued presence and experience of Jesus Christ in the church includes its transformation post-Easter, what keeps God's own identity from undergoing a similar transformation? This point of tension will be picked up and addressed later in more detail, but Haight's critique of *Logos* Christologies that, in affirming the humanity of Jesus, one ends up separating his humanity from our own, seems too appropriate for Bracken's Spirit Christology on this point.

One last wrinkle in Bracken's Christology that cannot help but be a strength or a weakness in the eyes of the reader is its picture of eschatological hope. If Creation is created out of the excess of love, an overflowing from the divine matrix that seeks to make space for an Other, if Creation comes out of the abyss of creativity at the beckoning of God's possibility-evoking-self-giving, and if this Creation has the kingdom of God not only as a momentary and fragile possibility, but as the consummation for which it was created—then, should all Creation come to receive and share in the divine life, our human subjectivities would cease to be the highest one. For Bracken, the Triune God is the "all-comprehensive system of divine communitarian life is both the transcendent origin and ultimate goal of the cosmic process as a vast network of dynamically interrelated and hierarchically ordered finite systems whose progressive growth in order and complexity began with the Big Bang and will ultimately end with full incorporation into the divine life."[88] Bracken's process Spirit Christology is one with eschatological premonitions of a moment in which all things have become subject to the Father so that God—the divine

---

87. Ibid., 255.
88. Ibid., 135.

matrix—may be all in all. One can see just how far Bracken has taken his neo-Whiteheadian philosophy. It is in the process of this development that he ends up leaving most of his fellow process thinkers behind, but when set alongside Haight, several possibilities arise.

Between Symbols and Systems

A few key points of comparison between Haight and Bracken will be examined intending to see what type of expanded richness we can develop. First, I will look at their understanding of postmodernity and theological method and the register in which they locate Christology, before turning to the specifics of their Spirit Christologies and articulation of the role of the Trinity. For Haight's postmodern apologetic Christology, the primary task is seeking to communicate to postmodern consciousness. While he points out that there is a cosmological consciousness at play, his own Spirit Christology is primarily determined by his interdisciplinary decision to use "symbol" as the centering concept and to develop a Christology from below, beginning with the historical Jesus. Bracken has not been timid when addressing the postmodern situation, even arguing that Derrida himself implied a metaphysics of becoming, thus for him metaphysics cannot be neglected.[89] Bracken consistently states that the progress toward a commonly accepted worldview is an essential part of fruitful dialogue. When it comes to methodological contrasts, they occur both when defining who the audience is and what the content is. For Bracken, the audience is not the general postmodern consciousness, but an audience who intends to both wrestle with questions of truth and seek a shared worldview. They both work across academic disciplines, but the expectations Bracken has for his audience are as fellow intellectuals. Perhaps the biggest tension between the two in their methodological commitments is theological—about the assumptive character of theology in general. For Haight, the reality of God is established through the experience of God, and those very experiences give the theology itself validity.[90] While revelation is a universal and subjective phenomenon, Haight sees the referent of this universal phenomenon to be accessible only through

---

89. Joseph A. Bracken, *The One in the Many: A Contemporary Reconstruction of the God-World Relationship* (Grand Rapids, MI: Eerdmans, 2001), 104-5.
90. Haight, *Dynamics of Theology*, 78-79.

one's own subjectivity.[91] The entire world is potentially revelatory, but it becomes such to the individual. This existential register to all theology, and especially in Christology, is essential and is not to be neglected. Given our postmodern context and the history of the church's cultural privilege, it is wise to acknowledge the contestability of God.[92] What Bracken adds to the conversation is a theological hesitation. He readily admits that the reality of God is a contestable statement, but rejects it being an optional affirmation for the Christian theologian. For Bracken, the reality of God centers the Christian faith and a plausible account of a real God who acts in the world is a necessary component of his Christology.[93] I do not think it is necessary for Open and Relational theologians to adhere to a particular account of the Trinity, but this contrast brings to the fore an important observation—namely that the existential register for Christology and much of the life of faith should not be cause for neglecting attention to other theological registers. The metaphysical register of an informed and credible affirmation of God is an important part of any Open and Relational theology. One reason is simply that, despite our postmodern situation, the question about the reality of God has not gone away. But even more, at the heart of an Open and Relational theology are the relationships themselves. Bracken here insists that the Christian conception of God is one who acts, and he adds that actions require God to be more than a force or ground, but also analogous to human agents.[94] There is a difference between the divine and human agency given that God has no point of origin, but by appropriating the systems-oriented approach, there can be an analogy of becoming between the Creator and creatures. This metaphysical contrast, as we have seen, has purchase for Christology.

Both Haight and Bracken insist that the life of faith is one mediated through Jesus. Likewise, they insist that the same Spirit that animated the life of Jesus should and could do so now for contemporary believers. In part, this means that the particularities of Jesus' living out of his mission and ministry are models for us as we face contemporary challenges. These two different Spirit Christologies share a feature interpretative insight, mainly that it was the human

---

91. Ibid., 56-61.
92. Taylor, *A Secular Age*, 675, 727.
93. Bracken, "Panentheism," 207-8, 224-25.
94. Bracken, *The World in the Trinity*, 85-86.

Jesus' faithfulness to God which, in part, made possible God's presence in and God's work through him. When compared to theologies that seek to locate the necessary perfection of Jesus' humanity by protecting him from sin, this turn from sinlessness to faithfulness is welcomed. Here it recognizes that the full humanity of Jesus can be affirmed and, leaving behind biological accounts of original sin, our own humanity receives new dignity. As mentioned above, there is some concern that Bracken's depiction of the human subjectivity of Jesus undercuts this theological potential. I would argue that Bracken's depiction of how the higher-order divine subjectivity operates with Jesus' human subjectivity neglects the synoptic narrative's depiction of Jesus' own growth and development in relationship to the one he called Abba. Not only is there a growth depicted in Luke's narration of the adolescent Jesus in Jerusalem, but it is seen in encounters in his ministry such as his conversation with the Syrophoenician Woman and in each of the Baptism narratives we see a new experience with God take place. The baptism is not the beginning of Jesus' Spirit-filled experience of God, because he sought John out at the Jordan, but it was a heightening of his Abba experience. The nurturing presence of God characterizes the life of Jesus both before and after his vocational call, but even affirming an unbroken communion with God need not deny growth and development. For humans, growth and development are part of the dignity of being human. For an Open and Relational theologian, that we are created to live in a dynamic relationship with God, neighbor, and world is both essential and the very location in which we live out our faith. For this reason, we lose something when the human subjectivity of Jesus is made subject to his divine subjectivity. The dynamic of reliance and openness, both of dependency and empowerment in God, were part of Jesus' experience in the synoptic gospels all the way to the prayer in Gethsemane. The faithfulness of Jesus as empowered by the Spirit that sets Jesus apart. In the conclusion of this text, my resistance to Bracken's seeming subsumption of Jesus' own human subjectivity into the eternal Son's divine subjectivity will be further developed. It is important to note here that Haight's more robust account of human subjectivity and the nature of human freedom must be included in an open and relational account. Haight's Irenaean depiction of Jesus includes the growth, development, and struggle intrinsic to human existence. The full humanity of Jesus compels me to locate this growth within Jesus' own life and not have it established at the outset. I will discuss later the consequences for the Trinity and the work of God in Christ. For now, I just want to emphasize that Bracken's cosmological picture shared by most open and relational theologians is such that a new emergent reality, one that is qualitatively new with the power to exercise top-down causation, need not have an eternal correspondent in the mind of God to emerge. Even then, a new element of emergent complexity in the story of the cosmos remains a product of the God-World relationship. Perhaps the life of Jesus is the place in which a deeper fusion of God and World occurred.

My primary concern here is pursuing the possibility of a Spirit Christology that affirms both the fullness of Jesus' humanity and the fullness of God's presence in Jesus. If Jesus' humanity includes the process of growth and development akin to all humans, Jesus' faithfulness becomes a way to understand his contribution to the process. It's just that the process is not his and his alone. As mentioned in the introduction, the three elements of power that go into each moment of becoming are the inheritance of the past, the gift of possibility, and the responsibility of freedom. If Jesus was fully faithful to the call of the Spirit in each ever kenotic, self-emptying moment, surely there would have been growth and development. Over the course of his life, the inheritance of the past grew deeper, making new depths of fidelity possible through him. Delineating these powers here in a Spirit Christology is important for when you look at all three elements of a moment of becoming, the Spirt-filled fidelity of Jesus is also the result of God's faithfulness and the result of God's own investment in the world and in the life of Jesus. The power of an Open and Relational Spirit Christology is not simply the ability to begin from below with the person of Jesus, but also to recognize that through the work of the Spirit the faith-fullness of Jesus gave existence to God's insistence in each moment of his life. In Christ, God is present not simply through inspiration nor possession, but also in empowerment. This empowerment is expressive of the one whom Jesus called *Abba*, but the empowerment is not simply regarding Jesus. After the resurrection, the church came to understand itself to be part of this empowerment of the Spirit. They were charged to let the same kenotic mind of Christ dwell in them, for the faithfulness of Jesus was not simply exemplar, but participatory. Because God was in Christ and continues to be through the Spirit, the Christian community participates in the reality of Jesus' established fidelity. Just as the disciples' relationship with Jesus was sustained yet transformed through the resurrection, so too was God's relationship to the believing community and perhaps to the world. Jesus' faithfulness was much more than a model; it was God's divine self-investment in the world.

4

FROM SPIRIT TO *LOGOS*

The church's Christological reflection has included several conceptual starting points. When it comes to those concepts or images that center on the person of Jesus, none have been more important than the concept of the *Logos*. While the opening prologue to the Gospel of John gives the concept center stage, this is not the only reason the early church used it so frequently. Within the New Testament itself, it is the image from the Gospels in which the divine identity of Jesus precedes anything particular to the historical person Jesus. Theologically speaking, it is only by connecting the person of Jesus to the *Logos* that the one who is called the Son of God in the narratives themselves is understood to have always been the Son of God. The cosmic scope of the *Logos* relocates the soundscape of the Jesus story itself beyond his own mission to Israel.

The centrality of the *Logos* is not simply seen in its place within the New Testament. The affirmation of the pre-existence of the Son would have remained problematic if the narrative and symbolic backdrop of the church remained predominately Jewish in origin. Through the introduction of Hellenistic imagery found in the *Logos* and Wisdom tradition, there is an escalation of the scale and scope of the Christological affirmation about Jesus. When the Father and Son are one as seen in John's gospel, there is no longer divine activity apart from the Son all the way from creation to consummation. This concept found in John's Gospel has a history much bigger than the evangelist imagined. By the time the battle between Athanasius and Arius ended, the *Logos* had a lengthy history, which the church is still yet to shake. In this second chapter reflecting on the person of Jesus, I will argue that we need not shake loose of the contested image of the *Logos*, but attend to it again, raising attention to some historic debates and then turn to the *Logos* for a new word. This chapter and its eventual proposal is being developed with an ear toward the concerns that both Haight and Bracken leveled against the tendencies of *Logos* Christologies—centrally that the language is too abstract and metaphysical and thus loses contact with the historical Jesus and especially that it neglects the ministry of Jesus.

In this chapter, I intend to compare the Christologies of Kathryn Tanner and John Cobb regarding the connection between their understandings of both salvation and universal history. They have both developed robust *Logos* Christologies in which God's relationship to the world, the nature of human beings, and the work of Christ are understood within and not apart from the incarnation. While some theologians will locate the redemptive event on the cross as their starting point, Cobb and Tanner both lead with the incarnation. Beyond the immediate contrasts, what remains striking is the distinctively similar account of God's intentions for the world that they both share. Both Tanner and Cobb use the Johannine understanding of the *Logos* for much more than a symbolic latch to connect the person of Jesus to God. Their shared insistence is that the incarnation serves as a key for understanding God's presence, activity, desire, and dream for the world. In divergent but powerful ways, they each see God's participation in the life of Jesus as a unique, particular, and transformative event for both God and the world. For both theologians, the incarnation of God is about all of Creation and not simply revelatory of Jesus. Revealed in Christ is both the model of and means to participate in the divine life. Broadly, it is the contrasts about the nature of divine participation they both develop that will occupy this investigation's focus. In particular, it is the nature of divine self-investment in and through the *Logos* which will be primary.

Participation from Weak to Strong

Kathryn Tanner is among the most creative and lucid contemporary theologians. In her Christology, *Christ the Key*, you see what she terms "historically funded Christian theology" in action. She reads the richness of the Christian tradition with its questions, concerns, and imaginative insights, in light of the contemporary situation to shake up, reorient, and expand the Church's theological and ethical imagination. It is here in her Christology where she truly embodies this vision and demonstrates its vitality by developing a robust incarnational Christology that is anything but a trivial recapitulation of the tradition.

At the heart of Tanner's work is a simple but profound thesis—namely, that God desires to give humanity the fullness of God's own life in the deepest way possible—through Christ. For Tanner, Christ is the key in a very specific way. It is through God's participation with us and for us in the hypostatic union that all of humanity comes to participate and share in the divine life. The nature of the human, Trinity, God-World relationship, atonement, and many other theological topics are developed out of this central thesis such that her account of the incarnation reveals more than simply her Christology. The narrative that Christian theology proclaims is one in which God, in each stage of the drama, represents "a greater communication of goodness to the creature and the overcoming of any sinful opposition to these gifts' distribution."[1] Strikingly, what is being communicated here is not clarity but goodness. For Tanner, this goodness is found in the divine life and comes through divine participation, which is God's self-gifting of the divine life to the world.

No concept in Tanner's account has as much interpretive power as participation. Throughout her description, the work of the Cappadocian Fathers and particularly Gregory of Nyssa play an essential role. From them she can appropriate a modified Platonist vision of participation in which all particular human beings participate in the human being par excellence—that is, Jesus Christ the image of God. In contrast to a more traditional Platonist scheme, a strict ontological divide is placed between the Creator and the creaturely reality. Because there is a strict dichotomy between the two, there cannot be "an ontological continuum spanning the difference between God and creatures."[2] Instead, it is the Christological commitments fashioned in response to the Arian controversy that reveal a two-fold participatory relationship between the creature and their Creator, both of which take the eternal Son as their origin. The Son is both the Word from whom all creation comes and the incarnate one in whom the perfect union and image of God is given to the world. Creaturely existence, which is composite and has being only through participation in that which it is not, leads Tanner to distinguish between weak and strong participation, both of which are divine works of grace originating in the Son.

---

1. Kathryn Tanner, *Jesus, Humanity and the Trinity: A Brief Systematic Theology* (Minneapolis, MN: Fortress, 2003), 2.

2. Kathryn Tanner, *Christ the Key* (Cambridge: Cambridge University Press, 2010), 18.

Weak participation is our givenness as a creature of God brought forth from the Word. Prior to the act of creation, what we receive preexists in God the Word and our coming into being is then a movement that originates in God. This makes our image-bearing identity something that we do not possess, but something that is derived from our participation in the Word, which is the image of the invisible and incomprehensible God. While not our own, this weak form of participation is part of our created identity before God. Thus, strong participation in Tanner's mind is our coming to participate in what we are not — namely God. This intense form of participation took place and was made possible through the incarnation in Jesus Christ. Here in this human being, God was redemptively present uniquely with a universal horizon. As Tanner puts it, "Jesus, in so far as he is divine, does not just have the divine image within himself through participation but is it."[3] In Christ, his humanity shared fully in the derivative dignity of humanity in its weak participation, and yet because of Christ's divinity, God's own being was given as shared with humanity as a whole. Through the Word's incarnation, "the Word has us in a new way and that means we can have the Word in a new way" beyond the previously available possibilities.[4] The hypostatic union is the means by which the ontological gap between the Creator and God's creatures is bridged. This makes the life of Jesus more than a model of the perfectly faithful human being, but also saves his life from being relegated to the neglected preface of God's redemption through the cross and resurrection. Through the dynamism of her two forms of participation, she can follow Athanasius, who saw that the Word is known through his work both in the act of creation and redemption. In Augustinian fashion, the eyes of faith are necessary to see the incomprehensible God who was present in Jesus. In fact for Tanner, seeing in faith does not mean comprehension, but participation in being one with Christ, for: "incomprehensible in his divinity, we take on the very incomprehensibility of the divine rather than simply running after it, working to reproduce it in human terms."[5] Through the union of both humanity and divinity in the one human Jesus, he thus becomes both the pattern and the cause of a new form of reconciled human life - a human life that participates by grace in the divine life.

---

3. Ibid., 35.
4. Ibid., 36.
5. Ibid., 56.

It is an important observation to note that while Tanner appropriates many of the classical Christological formulations, a nuanced re-authoring takes place. By both occupying the language of the tradition and giving it new life, she can demonstrate the reservoir of meaning lurking under the catacombs of theology. There is a temptation for those who do Christian theology with an eye toward contemporary ethical and methodological challenges to dismiss the theological resources that Tanner harnesses to address these very problems.[6] Her work here demonstrates the need for contemporary theologians to hesitate longer before jettisoning the hypostatic union from the theological tongue. In fact, across her different works, Tanner regularly draws our attention to "what Christians want to say" through the oddities of Christian grammar.[7] We see a narrative theological thread in her concept of participation that runs through her understanding of Creation, Anthropology, Incarnation, and Salvation.

The narrative of participation begins with the ontological distinction between the Creator and the creature established by God's free decision to create ex nihilo. This metaphysical doctrine functions as an axiological affirmation of the value of creation—namely weak participation. Regardless of a particular entity's complexity, everything that has its being has received its being from God and thus participates, albeit weakly, in God. This also means that Tanner's anthropology is not stuck asking how to get the spiritual into the material, but how to describe the uniqueness of humanity such that through its openness, relationality, dignity, and plasticity, it can come to receive the presence of God.[8] This anthropological particularity, historically described as the *Imago Dei*, is not something inserted into human beings making them an exception in creation, but is an intensification and expression of the very purpose of creation.[9] The Incarnation is then a perfect enactment of the very capacities that all creatures share "elevated through the gift of the Holy Spirit" in order for Christ to conform to the image of the eternal Word.[10] Because the narrative being spun is one of participation, the site of salvation is the incarnation itself,

---

6. For example, in the text itself Tanner directly addresses the feminist criticisms of Western atonement theories while doing a constructive theology of the cross.

7. Carl S. Hughes, "'Tehomic' Christology? Tanner, Keller, and Kierkegaard on Writing Christ," *Modern Theology* 31, no. 2 (2015): 260.

8. Tanner, *Christ the Key*, 41.

9. Ibid., 28.

10. Ibid., 25.

for in this event, and not before, the Word both has us as creatures in a new way and creates the conditions for us to have the Word in a new way.[11] This means that Tanner describes grace primarily as an expansion of our nature as image bearers of God established for salvation at creation and opened and connected through our weak participation.

Grace upon Grace

Having established both forms of human participation in God as derivative from the Son, it follows that her Christology would be centered in an exploration of the nature of grace. Here the intricacy of her groundbreaking account comes to the fore. One way of setting the stage for the contribution of her work is by considering how she can weave the Christological concerns of the Cappadocians together with the Reformers. The centrality of grace for Christology is vintage Protestantism, yet her incarnational approach allows her to nest it within the cosmological frame of the Cappadocians. How she accomplishes this becomes clear in her account of the human predicament.

For Tanner, it is nature and not sin that is the primary place of departure for understanding the character of grace. Human beings are images of God by grace and not by nature. This difference is important for distinguishing humanity from the eternal Son and incarnate Christ. Only Christ is the image of God by nature and we were created to participate in God. The human predicament is not then our failure to live up to the potential that was rightfully ours in our own nature, namely being a sinner before God. Humans "cannot be the image in virtue of the human nature with which we were created. Grace is necessary to make us strong images of God because our nature as human creatures is incapable of doing so."[12] Our coming to participate strongly in the divine life happens through God's own free loving initiative present in our creation through the Word and redemption through the incarnation. It is hard to exaggerate how this shift in understanding of the human predicament from sin to nature transforms her account of grace. The problem is not humanity's fallen status because of our participation in sinful humanity. Grace is not God's creative response to a failed and fallen project. Instead, we are given grace

---

11. Ibid., 36.
12. Ibid., 59.

through our originating status as beings from God created to live before God. One could say that Tanner's redemption story from creation to consummation could be summed up as 'grace upon grace.'

The removal of sin is not key to the Christological metanarrative of grace, it is God's initiative and intention to bring a creature into existence who could come to participate in God's essence. The predicament in which the grace of God's strong participation with us in Christ is best understood, is that humans are not divine and yet created for it. As Tanner puts it plainly in connecting the two works of grace, "humans have to be given God in addition to being given themselves" and it is in Christ that both God and humanity are one, so "the grace of God in Christ becomes the highest way of addressing the impediment to God's design posed by creation, irrespective of any problem of sin."[13] It is important to note here how Tanner's account of grace does not require sin to create the conditions for its coming. In differentiating her grace-laden account from the Catholic view of the nature-grace relationship, she restates the function of grace by distinguishing it from a continuum view. In a world where sin is present, there can exist a continuum between humans and their natural responsiveness to God, yet "there cannot be any such continuum between God and creatures. Grace that takes the form of the gift of God's own presence is for this reason never anything less than unexacted."[14] Human nature cannot exist apart from grace, and its coming is not a supplement to what was already present precisely because it was created from and for grace - participation in God. The human, even one in sin, is not in the process of overcoming what they have become to become what they are not. The human is in the process of receiving the fullness of the divine life that God chooses to freely give in Christ. Here one becomes exactly what one is: God's. Human nature differs then from other animals because its nobility comes not from being itself apart from God but by being itself before God. It is constitutive of our very nature to adhere to the goodness of God, for our ultimate value depends on something outside ourselves.[15]

If human nature is given in grace and completed in grace, specific attention needs to be given as to how both acts of grace are given. On multiple occasions,

---

13. Ibid., 60.
14. Ibid., 133.
15. Ibid., 139.

Tanner uses a helpful distinction by differentiating between conceptions of
participation that inhere within the human and those that adhere. Even in the
above discussion about humanity's weak participation in God as creatures,
Tanner consistently wants all our goodness to come from adhering to God. The
distinction being employed in Tanner's account of our created status serves to
emphasize the nature of grace, but more than that it enables her to make the
connection between the Cappadocians and the Reformers more robust. By
centering the story of redemption on the transformation of human nature rather
than the conquering of sin, Tanner is echoing the theological heartbeat of
Gregory of Nyssa, and yet this peculiar grace-laced account enables her to speak
it in the accent of Luther.

In Tanner's telling of both creation and redemption, the divine is being
given to us so that it must never "become some kind of 'inherent form,' some
odd but still human quality of a supernaturally elevated sort." No, it "remains
the power of the divinity itself, made ours by clinging to what we are not. Rather
than being inherent in us, this power merely adheres to us in virtue of that
clinging."[16] The goodness given by the Word in creation and redemption is
properly alien to us as the pure gift of divine participation. Grace is not the result
of a process with incremental improvement but is rather a disjunctive leap to a
different condition. Just as the creature is given her existence in a free decision
of grace from God, so too is our redemption an act of God's grace that brings us
what we lack by nature. Humans are no more responsible for their recreation in
Christ than they are for their creation from the Word. Our divinity is always
external to our nature as an adherent to our being that comes from God by grace.
By making that which is divine in the human an adherent, our human nature
remains unchanged under the effects of sin. Our corruption is not the corruption
of what we were, but the loss of what we are not.[17] Here her previously
developed anthropology that emphasized a natural openness, malleability, and
plasticity in the world bears much theological fruit. Thus, the question follows:
if sin does not entail the transformation of human nature, to what is sin directed?
Tanner's answer is that the status of the divine power within us is the focus. By
locating sin's distorting effects in our environment, "our operations are
corrupted because sin alters what is available in our

---

16. Ibid., 104.
17. Ibid., 65.

surroundings for our proper nourishment. With no disease or damage to our natural capacities, we are poisoned or polluted from without, because of what we have done to the only environment suitable for us."[18] If the human is by nature in need of divine nourishment, a different environment substantially alters the human's relationship with both God and the World without altering human nature.[19] In this way, Tanner can affirm both total depravity and the preservation of our created nature despite sin.

The last observation to make about the nature of Tanner's grace-led Christology is how the incarnation of God in Christ can transform our human nature. Tanner is clear that "the incarnation is for the sake of human redemption," which means it is "not to give the Word a human shape but to bring about an altered manner of human existence, one realizing on the human plane the very mode of existence of the second person of the trinity."[20] The incarnation ultimately serves neither a pedagogical intention of God nor a preparatory purpose, but is instead "the primary mechanism of atonement."[21] Thus, humanity as sinful through the hardening of our hearts to God's influence becomes closed off to God. Our weak participation in God is weakened as we more openly embrace our sin-filled environment, and sin's influence on the individual is dramatic. Tanner adds that sin's solution is not a return to a more open human nature through a renewal of our weak participation, but the new way in which the Word and Spirit are ours in Christ. For this reason, the human needs from God precisely what it cannot do for itself in two respects. The human needs both its sinful context changed so it can freely love God, and it remains in need of a new nature so it may participate in God. The hypostatic union is thus the context in which Tanner sees both acts take place. In Christ, the attachment of humanity to the divine is closer, stronger, and categorically different from that which is available to the human nature alone. Jesus' relationship to the divine is not simply one of radical human faithfulness and devotion to the divine, but is instead humanity's assumption "into the unity with the second person of the trinity to form a single person; a hypostatic union."[22] To be clear about the nature of the divine initiative in the incarnation, Tanner

---

18. Ibid., 68.
19. Ibid., 42.
20. Ibid., 147.
21. Ibid., 252.
22. Ibid., 71.

emphasizes how hypostatic unity is a precondition for the life of Jesus and the means by which both sin's influence can be negated and the human nature transformed. Because it is precisely God acting in Christ, all of humanity is transformed. Tanner compares the gain that humanity makes through Christ as comparable to the natural connection that the Word enjoys with other members of the trinity. Because Christ is attached to us in virtue of the humanity he shares with us, we also share in the divinity that he participates in. Justification then is "a matter of the incarnation and of the divine powers possessed by the humanity of Christ in virtue of that unity with the Word. Sanctification refers to what happens to the humanity of Christ on that basis over the course of his life and death."[23] We thus receive in Christ the gift of God's own life and its impact both justifies us and enables us to participate in Jesus' own sanctification. Tanner's vision has this thoroughly Protestant chant of grace, and yet it is amplified through connecting to the cosmic vision of the Cappadocians. The individual Christian indeed comes to know God through God's benefits and yet God's gracious intention has always been to give all creatures the fullness of God's own life, and it is this story that swallows sin, defeats death, and transforms our nature.

Narrating Divine Self-Investment

Tanner gives a specific shape in her rendering of the Christian narrative that emphasizes the nature of divine self-investment. The story of God and Creation moves through a series of stages, each bringing the world a greater share in the divine life. As she puts it, "each stage of this history—creation, covenant, salvation in Christ—represent(s) a greater communication of goodness to the creature and the overcoming of any sinful opposition to these gifts' distribution."[24] In light of her Platonist conception of the Good, this rendering of the Christian narrative is not just the story of communicating goodness, but of increasing participation in the divine life itself. What is being communicated by Tanner is not some content or truth about God, but God in Godself. For this reason, the incarnation of the Word of God is the central theological doctrine. Here Tanner echoes Karl Barth's reflection on the relationship of world history

---

23. Ibid., 99.
24. Tanner, *Jesus, Humanity and the Trinity*, 2.

and divine governance when he identifies Christ as "the centre and key to all events" and yet it is the incarnation and not the cross which is her hinge of history.[25] Tanner's contention is that the world is being perfected as it is brought into closer relations with the perfecting God, and the event that made that a reality was the Word becoming flesh.[26]

While the narration of divine participation centers here on the incarnation, Tanner is clear that the incarnation is not a form of divine invasion. Throughout her work, she has sought to develop a non-competitive understanding of divine action. In this way, one can affirm that God was in Christ without abrogating the integrity of Creation or making God responsible for the reality of evil. Far from abrogating Creation, God is thus present by grace in, through, and to all Creation throughout its history. This weak participation in God which is the ontological dignity of Creation has a unique plasticity and openness in the human creature such that the incarnational affirmation confessed in the hypostatic union is, in fact, anything but static. When Tanner explicitly lays out the "meaning of the hypostatic union" she says that "Jesus is the one who lives in God, the one who is all that he is as a human being without existing independently of God, the human being whose very existence is God's own existence."[27]

Cobb's Constructive Theology in the Key of Whitehead

John Cobb's theology not only develops from the philosophical vision of Whitehead, but he also takes Whitehead's theological intuitions seriously. In *Religion in the Making*, Whitehead recognized that part of Christianity's genius is that it "points at the facts and asks for their systematic interpretation."[28] Later in *The Adventures of Ideas*, Whitehead is highly critical of liberal Christians who gave up on systematic and rational thought in light of the 18th

---

25. Karl Barth, *The Doctrine of Creation*, §§ 48-49, Church Dogmatics, study edition 19, ed. Geoffrey William. Bromiley and Thomas F. Torrance, vol. 3 pt. 3 (London: T & T Clark, 2010), 190.

26. Tanner, *Jesus, Humanity and the Trinity*, 2.

27. Kathryn Tanner, "Eschatology Without a Future?" in *The End of the World and the Ends of God*, ed. John Polkinghorne and Michael Welker (Harrisburg, PA: Trinity, 2000), 230.

28. Whitehead, *Religion in the Making*, 51.

and 19th century.[29] In his mind, the real threat that theology faced was 'the doctrine of dogmatic finality' and instead many gave up on what Whitehead identified as the essence of Christianity, namely "the appeal to the life of Christ as a revelation of the nature of God and of his agency in the world."[30] These few remarks move toward a theological methodology that is not bound by the limits of historical scholarship and scientism alone, but finds new possibilities when 'facts' and 'essence' of the faith are developed in a metaphysical vision that is more compatible with the faith in Cobb's mind. Whitehead's adventurous spirit is present throughout Cobb's thought and can especially be seen in his theological engagement of new challenges and situations.

Before turning to Cobb's Process Christology, it is important to understand how Cobb understands the concept of God in Whitehead's philosophy. For Whitehead, nothing just exists, but everything grows together. Everything grows out of datum, and the datum themselves had their own process of becoming; so for Whitehead, "it belongs to the nature of a 'being' that it is a potential for every becoming."[31] God plays an essential role in the world's becoming by being the "actual entity imposing its own unchanged consistency of character on every phase" so that "a definite result is emergent" from the process.[32] In *Religion in the Making*, Whitehead recognized that this made God an actual but non-temporal entity which must include "a synthesis of the total universe," such that there is a part of God where the realm of forms is qualified by the world and where the world is qualified by the forms.[33] As his thought developed in *Process and Reality*, he came to describe God as having two natures. First, he describes the primordial nature, which orders the eternal objects for the attainment of value in the temporal world and the consequent nature, which receives the temporal world into God. God's di-polarity enables God to feel, know, preserve, and save the world. As Cobb points out, God saves the world by transforming the world.[34]

29. Alfred North Whitehead, *The Adventures of Ideas* (New York: The Free Press, 1933), 162.
30. Ibid., 167.
31. Ibid., 22.
32. Whitehead, *Religion in the Making*, 94.
33. Ibid., 98.
34. John B. Cobb Jr., *A Christian Natural Theology: Based on the Thought of Alfred North Whitehead*, 2nd ed. (Louisville, KY: Westminster John Knox, 2007), 102.

Whitehead recognized the necessity of God's presence for becoming when he said, "apart from the intervention of God, there could be nothing new in the world, and no order in the world. The course of creation would be a dead level of ineffectiveness, with all balance and intensity progressively excluded by the cross currents of incompatibility."[35] As both the ordering ground for the becoming of the world and the freedom enabling ground for its creatures, God is a constitutive part of each actual occasion. In addition to the experience of the past actual world, each becoming includes an experience of God. It is important to note that this experience of God is essential for temporal existence but that it does not require a subjective awareness. Each moment of becoming is experiencing God, even if the occasion is not conscious of it.

Cobb contends that the role of God is 'creative' and 'absolutely essential', but it remains one among others.[36] Cobb points to Whitehead, who says that "each task of creation is a social effort, employing the whole universe."[37] The unique role of God is understood by Cobb to be that which makes creative response a possibility for the becoming of each event. God is understood to provide alternatives to each event in what is physically given to it and thus calls it toward realizing what is best for the given situation. God's activity is as a persuasive presence and not a compelling power, for "it is God's role to give freedom to that experience and responsibility as to how that freedom is used."[38] Though there are clear distinctions between the God-World relationship as understood in Cobb's thought and the contrasting dominant understanding in classical theology, he can still affirm that "God is the creator of every actual occasion and therefore of every actual entity other than God."[39] By recognizing that the initial phase of each occasion's subjective aim comes from God, he understands God as the principle of initiation in each event. That does not mean however that Cobb gives to God the sole status as 'ultimate.'

In discussing the relationship between creativity and God, Cobb concludes that the question of superiority is meaningless because they have no reality apart

---

35. Whitehead, *Process and Reality,* 247.
36. Cobb, *A Christian Natural Theology*, 113.
37. Whitehead, *Process and Reality*, 223.
38. John B. Cobb Jr., "Process Thought" in *Philosophy of Religion in the 21st Century,* ed. D. Z. Phillips and Timothy Tessin (New York: Palgrave, 2001), 258.
39. Cobb, *A Christian Natural Theology*, 115.

from each other.[40] In fact, God and creativity also need the world, but that does not lead one to question the hierarchy of existence once again. As Whitehead notes, "there is no meaning to 'creativity' apart from its 'creatures,' and no meaning to 'God' apart from 'creativity' and the 'temporal creatures,' and no meaning to the 'temporal creatures' apart from 'creativity' and 'God.'"[41] For Cobb, the persuasive nature of God's power is not chosen, but natural. The nature of reality is such that God has never been nor could have been coercive. God did not choose to limit Godself prior to creation, but "God and the World stand over against each other, expressing the final metaphysical truth that appetitive vision and physical enjoyment have an equal claim to priority in creation."[42] To say this does not make God less responsive and involved in the World and its history. On the contrary, "apart from him there could be no world, because there could be no adjustment of individuality."[43] The world is then saved from banality and repetition because God is always investing Godself in the world and becoming vulnerable to the diminishment of value and the intensification of its expression. On this, Cobb states, "God is the urge to adventure and the ground of the possibility of response."[44] It is here that Whitehead's philosophical vision can both inspire Cobb's natural theology and give the dynamic vision of God that Cobb finds to resonate so well with the Biblical witness.[45]

God after Omnipotence

For Cobb, the central task of Christian theology is a doctrine of God. Early in his career, he framed his constructive theology in light of two central observations. First, he states that what the God the Christian theologian seeks to articulate is the God of Jesus. And second, he notes that in the current situation, traditional theism's God is dead. For both, the question of divine power is important. Cobb articulates that omnipotence is a metaphysical compliment that has distracted the church from the God of Jesus, and has thus left God open to an unsurpassable protest in light of evil and suffering. Many

40. Cobb, *A Christian Natural Theology*, 118.
41. Whitehead, *Process and Reality*, 225.
42. Ibid., 348.
43. Whitehead, *Religion in the Making*, 158.
44. Cobb, *A Christian Natural Theology*, 141.
45. Ibid., 119.

theologians will rightly push back to Cobb's definition of omnipotence as a hyperbolic characterization of the tradition or perhaps insist that his critique is limited to more thorough-going forms of determinism in thinkers like John Calvin. Cobb does not deny this possibility, but points to how uncomfortable the defenders of omnipotence get when it is under attack. Either God could or could not have intervened to stop the tragic death of a child, and for Cobb, there is no way God's character is preserved with an 'unwilled could.' Regardless of the metaphysical explanation surrounding the affirmation of omnipotence, Cobb wants to turn the question away from philosophical parsing to the very character of God. Is God's character such that God had possibilities available that could have saved a child's life and did not actualize them? If so, this God does not cohere with the one Jesus called *Abba*. Remaining aware of how Cobb's inclusive yet narrow definition of omnipotence functions rhetorically can enable one to see just what Cobb believes is at stake.

Cobb's theological positioning is both Christocentric and insistent upon serious criticism of the Christian tradition. Both have their origin in the famous conclusion to Whitehead's *Process and Reality*, where he states:

> When the Western world accepted Christianity, Caesar conquered; and the received text of Western theology was edited by his lawyers. The code of Justinian and the theology of Justinian are two volumes expressing one movement of the human spirit. The brief Galilean vision of humility flickered through the ages, uncertainly. In the official formulation of the religion, it has assumed the trivial form of the mere attribution to the Jews that they cherished a misconception about their Messiah. But the deeper idolatry, of the fashioning of God in the image of the Egyptian, Persian, and Roman imperial rulers, was retained. The Church gave unto God the attributes which belonged exclusively to Caesar. [46]

In *God and the World*, Cobb developed the natural theology he previously worked out from Whitehead in *A Christian Natural Theology* and strived to make explicitly Christian constructive moves in his doctrine of God. Echoing Whitehead, he said that "now, as never before, we must allow what appeared in

---

46. Whitehead, *Process and Reality*, 342.

Jesus to give meaning and content to the Reality we thereby name."[47] As a liberal theologian, he inherited a suspicion of Hellenistic philosophy, but instead of retreating from metaphysical affirmations of God, divine action, and discussing the singularity of Jesus, Cobb adopted and appropriated process philosophy to develop a robust doctrine of God. And not only that, but Cobb also found that the process depiction of God as "an event, an occurrence of thinking, willing, feeling, and loving" was "closer to the heart of Biblical faith."[48] His process articulation of God has deep contrasts with classical theology which Cobb and his mentor, Charles Hartshorne, identified as resulting from the classical notion of divine perfection. When one switches from a philosophy that centers on Being to one that centers on Becoming, the very nature of divine perfection necessarily changes.

When it comes to divine power, Cobb saw several particular problems with omnipotence that center on the character of the God revealed in Jesus. For Cobb, classical theism's affirmation of God's omnipotence makes God responsible for everything that happens, and thus the evil present in the world remains a threat for affirming God's perfect goodness. When God's omnipotence is combined with God holding humanity accountable for its sin, you get what Cobb calls the "monstrous idea" God's justice holds humans responsible for sin for which God was ultimately responsible.[49] In addition, if God holds all the power, God's creatures hold none. Does God will evil? Does God permit evil? Rhetorically asking these questions, Cobb refuses to address the possibility that there is no genuine evil, which was already rejected in Whitehead's thought. Likewise, he insists that if God already determined and knew each moment, any sense of responsibility is illusionary and thus a challenge to the very impulse of Jesus' invitation into the reign of God.[50] The dynamic pictures of the God-World relationship seen in scripture between God and the people of Israel and the disciples and the one Jesus called *Abba* is far from the 'monstrous idea.' It assumes openness, relationship, and responsibility, and it is also grounded in the God who has revealed Godself to be love. Within his process theology, God is understood to be the source of this gift of

---

47. John B. Cobb Jr., *God and the World* (Eugene, OR: Wipf and Stock, 2000), 37.
48. Ibid., 72.
49. Ibid., 88.
50. John B. Cobb Jr., "A Process Concept of God," *in Concepts of the Ultimate,* ed. Linda J. Tessier (London: McMillan, 1989), 40-41.

responsibility and freedom. Thus, God is the one who comes to each moment and gracefully offers possibilities that are neither contained by what is already present nor pure repetitions of the past.

God known as the source of possibility and the originator of novelty shows a certain power, but it differs from the one Cobb sees in classical thought. In fact, he has even stated that the classical definition of omnipotence renders to God very little power, for where there is no competing power omnipotence means very little. When divine power is understood as the ability to compel and coerce, it corresponds to a parent who has been pushed to their wit's end and forces compliance from her child. In this scenario, the parent uses external power to intervene and coerce her child when she has failed to persuade her child and guide her child to do the best. Thus, coercion is evidence that the parent lacks the power she truly wants, for "the exercise of this kind of power can kill, but it cannot quicken." [51] To model divine power off an inferior form of human power is problematic, especially when one observes the degree to which the coercion exercised corresponds to the coerced one's powerlessness. Understanding divine power as persuasive rather than controlling is, for Cobb, the more effective depiction of what we experience and is thus more appropriate for drawing analogies to divine power.[52]

Cobb regularly uses the parental model in developing his understanding of divine power and action because it connects the Biblical image of the God Jesus prioritized, Abba, with the relational function of God in each moment of becoming. This understanding of power is grounded in love; for one does not seek to control the ones they love, but to share life with them and work together to bring the best into the world. If one sees persuasion as the more robust vision of power, Cobb says that "we may still use the term 'omnipotent' if we like but its meaning is quite altered" such that instead of a divine "monopoly of power" God "exercises the optimum persuasive power in relation to whatever is."[53] Because of the common assumptions about God's omnipotence, Cobb never pursues rehabilitating the word itself, but works to draw a sharp contrast in his rendering of divine power.

51. Cobb, *God and the World,* 89.
52. John B. Cobb Jr. and David Ray Griffin, *Process Theology: An Introductory Exposition* (Louisville, KY: Westminster John Knox, 1976), 29.
53. Cobb, *God and the World,* 90.

Cobb's revisioning of divine power through a process philosophy affects other classical notions of divine perfection. In Whitehead's philosophy, both essence and existence are included in actuality, which is more inclusive than these abstractions. When he uses the word 'perfect', he is referring to God as an actual entity. And when becoming is given interpretive priority, God is no longer understood as immutable, for God's consequent nature is constitutively tied to both the world and its duration. Again, as in the discussion of divine power, Cobb highlights the theological conclusions this alternative account opens up by looking at prayer. Nothing is more common to Christian piety than prayer to God, but one wonders what purpose prayer serves if God's perfection keeps God distant from change and the influence of the world. Surely some practices of prayer primarily function to change the attitude and disposition of the one praying, but the most common type of prayer among Christians is intercessory prayer. In intercessions, the one who prays calls out to God on behalf of another. In an intercessory prayer God, the person of concern, and the one(s) who pray are connected, and the expectation of this practice is that it creates the possibility for God to act in ways that were not available to God otherwise. Cobb's understanding of God is one in which God is always doing all God can do for the good and beautiful. What exactly God can do is determined by many factors that are not ultimately subject to God, so those who are receptive to God's call and faithful in response can increase the embodiment of God's will in a given moment. When you understand the world through a process vision, one is no longer connected only to those one knows or can touch, but to all creation such that intercessory prayer can be an activity in which the connection between creatures and their relationship to God is intensified. Whitehead developed this type of particular providence at the end of *Process and Reality* in the abstract and can apply to much more than prayer.[54] For Cobb, God is not the unmoved mover but the most moved mover, for what is immutable for God is God's character. Perfect love is demonstrated differently depending on the situation, as it is a vulnerable risk that has no life out of

---

54. In *Process and Reality,* Whitehead states, "But the principle of universal relativity is not to be stopped at the consequent nature of God. This nature itself passes into the temporal world according to its gradations of relevance to the various concrescent occasions… In the fourth phase the creative action completes itself. For the perfected actuality passes back into the temporal world, and qualifies this world so that each temporal actuality includes it as an immediate fact of relevant experience… It is the particular providence for particular occasions" (350-51).

relationships. And thus it holds that in a process world, divine perfection means that God would necessarily change because of God's relationships. Beyond God's immutability, Cobb's theology also challenges God's impassability and omniscience. Classically, omniscience has meant that God knew all things completely in their fullness. For Cobb, because duration is as real for God as it is for creation, there are distinct types of knowledge. God knows the past completely as past, is present as a fully aware participant in the present moment of becoming, and knows the future completely as future possibilities. The future is not a set and determined series of actions that have already been decided and determined, but the future comes to the present as possibilities not yet decided. Given the relational nature within process thought, the possibilities present to a future are clearer to God the more immediate they are, like the visibility provided by a flashlight at night. As for God's impassability, from early on Christian theologians sensed that the suffering of God was problematic given that change for God was questionable. On the other hand, central to the story of Jesus is the suffering and death of Jesus on the cross. Within Process thought, God's perfection is not preserved by keeping God from suffering. In fact, God completely shares, experiences, saves, and preserves each moment of experience. That is why Whitehead called God the "great companion - fellow sufferer who understands."[55] The cross of Jesus is not only something that God completely shares, but like all the crosses in history, on top of sharing in the suffering of God's creatures, God is the "victim of man's age-long resistance to the call to love his neighbor as himself."[56] This reality and its revelation through the cross of Jesus matters when examining the problem of evil; for there is no evil that God does not know completely and share in completely.[57]

At this point, it is important to highlight just how Cobb develops the theological description of evil and creation in Whitehead. First, when Cobb calls the world God's creation, he does so without affirming *creatio ex nihilo*.[58] Cobb finds this classical doctrine of creation being necessitated by God's omnipotence, not by scripture. In fact, he regularly highlights its absence within both the canon and many of the church's earliest theologians. In the different

---

55. Ibid., 351.
56. Cobb, *God and the World,* 97.
57. Ibid.
58. Cobb and Griffin, *Process Theology*, 65.

creation texts within scripture, one gets a very different picture than the omnipotent deity that creates by divine fiat. Rather, scripture puts forth an account of a God who creatively invests in Genesis' deep to bring life-supporting structures into being and then begins to work with and through the creation itself to bring forth life. Of course, in Whitehead the relationship of God and the World is co-eternal, but the development of structures that support what we now call creation today was not. As both the source of order and novelty, God is invested in the world in each moment of becoming. This dynamic relationship with the world brings about the adventure of the world. What begins as just ideal possibilities within the divine mind become possible actualities because of God's ongoing creative relationship with the World. From moment to moment, the world and its present order is both sustained by God and lured toward greater complexity. Cobb uses the incarnation to evoke the nature of this self-investment when he says, "this creatively and responsively loving God is incarnately active in the present, bringing about immediate good based on activity in the past, and with the purpose to bring about greater good in the future—a greater good that will involve a fuller incarnation of the divine reality itself."[59] When one looks at creation in any given moment, one must recognize an eternal dynamism of co-creation in which God invests in the World as conditioned by its given situation, which is itself a result of God's earlier creative investment in the world.

The second theological development upon Whitehead's discussion of creation and evil being God's responsibility. Cobb argues that God is "responsible for evil but not indictable for it."[60] To unpack this, Cobb initially points to the conditions that make evil possible. If God is understood as the "factor in the universe that makes for novelty, life, intensity of feeling, consciousness, freedom, and in humanity for genuine concern for others, and which provides the measure of order which supports these," then in any situation where evil emerges, God is in some sense responsible but never its author.[61] Divine responsibility lies in the structures that God brought into being over time through divine self-investment. The issue is not that God intended any of these divinely-facilitated structures of increased complexity and power to be used for

---

60. Ibid., 69.
61. Cobb, *God and the World*, 96.

evil, but that despite knowing the freedom of the world, God chose to invest in it. God may always seek ever-higher values, but as the intensity for good increases, so too does the intensity of evil increase as a possibility.[62] This correlation includes more intrinsic and instrumental forms of good and evil, therefore, "increasing the freedom of creatures was risky business for God's part. But it was a necessary risk if there was ever to be the chance for greatness."[63] This makes God's indictability for evil more of an assessment of whether the possible joys and experiences of the complex world we find ourselves in that resulted from God's self-investment are worth the experiences of evil and suffering as well.

The *Logos* Liberally Applied

Cobb's natural theology is essential for understanding his Christology, precisely because throughout all his reflection about Jesus, the experience of Christ in the Christian community, and the relationship between God and Christ, he does not posit a form of divine intervention or supersession of reality. In fact, his Christology contains sharp criticism of the metaphysical tradition that necessitated metaphysical exceptions to affirm the incarnation. Cobb's Christological pattern is in holding with Whitehead's maxim about God, that neither God nor an affirmation of the incarnation of God in Christ should be an exemption from the structures of reality, but an intensification of them. To articulate his Christology, Cobb builds upon the God-World relationship described above, moving on both logically and sequentially from articulating God's presence in all things. He initially identifies Christ as the principle of creative transformation within Whitehead's philosophy. From there, he examines the uniqueness and particularity of Jesus and his ongoing presence in the world. This means that Cobb's method is also seen in his Christology as explicitly tied to his metaphysics, because it creates the conditions for the possibility of making any specific claim. The question remains whether or not it possesses more explanatory power than other formulations while responding to the contextual challenges of Christology today, but the contrasts here with Tanner are clear.

---

62. Ibid., 97.
63. Cobb and Griffin, *Process Theology,* 74.

The Christological point of departure for Cobb is his connection of the *Logos* Christology of the early church to the natural theology he developed out of Whitehead's philosophy. Like other *Logos* Christologies, Cobb's emphasis is on the incarnation, which permits a much more generous reading of other traditions and their relationship with God. For example, Justin Martyr can argue that both Abraham and Plato anticipated the coming of Christ as pre-Christ Christians.[64] Cobb differs from this tradition significantly in that the person of Jesus is not constitutively related to that which was present at previous enlightening moments of western history. Instead, the pre-existent *Logos* is here identified with the primordial nature of God in Whitehead. 'Christ' is seen as the particular possibilities for creative transformation that are available and actualized through the process of becoming.[65] By locating "Christ as the process itself," Cobb can identify any positive response to the lure of God with 'Christ' as creative transformation.[66] It follows then that, "Christ, as the image of creative transformation, can provide a unity within which the many centers of meaning and existence can be appreciated and encouraged and through which openness to the other great Ways of humanity can lead to a deepening of Christian existence."[67] This move is essential, but for Cobb, it is a faithful articulation of the intention of the church as it worked out the creedal formulas.[68] In Cobb's account, substance-based metaphysics ends up requiring a series of heretical suggestions when attempting to explain the hypostatic union in which some part of Jesus' humanity is usually replaced or overridden. There can be no solution by subtraction when it comes to the person of Jesus. For Cobb, there is no "metaphysical break radically separating Jesus from all other human beings," and yet Cobb does not end by simply naturalizing the incarnation.[69] As he puts it, "we could say in the most literal sense that every

---

64. Justin Martyr, *The First Apology, The Second Apology, Dialogue with Trypho, Exhortation to the Greeks, Discourse to the Greeks, The Monarchy or the Rule of God*, ed. and trans. Thomas B. Falls (Baltimore: Catholic University of America Press, 2011), 1 Apol. 46:3-4.
65. John B. Cobb Jr., *Christ in a Pluralistic Age* (Philadelphia: Westminster, 1975), 225.
66. Ibid., 15.
67. Ibid., 21.
68. Ibid., 169ff.
69. John B. Cobb Jr., "Christ Beyond Creative Transformation," in *Encountering Jesus: A Debate on Christology*, ed. Stephen David (Atlanta, GA: John Know, 1988), 144.

fleshly entity enfleshes or "incarnates" God. But we can also make even stronger claims about how God is present in Jesus."[70]

Cobb is sympathetic to those theologians who find it hard to say more about Jesus than identifying him as an example of an ideally responsive person to God's lure. Theologians who open themselves up to facing the contextual challenges of today, including the advent of historical criticism and the quest for the historical Jesus, are facing a difficult task. What then does Cobb mean when he says, "the 'Christ of faith' is continuous with the 'Jesus of history'"?[71] Knowing that he is thinking in a Process scheme where God is already in all things, the question then becomes: how are we to differentiate the presence of God in the 'Jesus of history' from other exceptional human beings? Cobb has not ignored the work of New Testament scholars and throughout his career, one can see him responding to different reconstructions; be it Schweitzer's apocalyptic prophet or the Jesus Seminar's cynic sage, yet for Cobb, it is "the image of Jesus shaped through the Gospels, not something behind them" that is of primary concern for the theologian.[72] A few near-consensus moments of historical scholarship, such as Jesus' radical intimacy with *Abba*, the remarkable authority with which he taught and forgave sin, and the powerful encounters he occasioned, create the backdrop for Cobb's investigation into the person of Jesus in which his faithfulness facilitates a co-constitution of his self-hood with God.

The *Abba*-intimacy of Jesus and his unsurpassed prophetic authority leads Cobb to ask, "What kind of structure of existence would give someone the ability to claim this distinctive form of authority?"[73] In short, Cobb contends that the initial aim co-constitutes the self, or "the I," of Jesus. God is incarnate in all events, but the incarnation of God is in Jesus' very self-hood. As such, Jesus is enabled "to focus not on his own experience of God but on others and the world...free from the distortion introduced by personal interests and ego defense."[74] The struggle for awareness and faithfulness to God that characterizes the human life, at least for some moments of Jesus life, did not

---

70. John B. Cobb Jr., *Theological Reminiscences* (Claremont, CA: Process Century, 2014), 282.

71. John B. Cobb Jr., "Jesus and Christ in Process Perspective," in *Handbook of Process Theology*, ed. Donna Bowman (St. Louis, MO: Chalice, 2006), 29.

72. John B. Cobb Jr., conversation with author, December 2, 2009.

73. Ibid.

74. Cobb, "Jesus and Christ in Process Perspective," 146.

define his structure of existence. Instead, Jesus' self was co-constituted by the prehension of both Jesus' personal history and the prehension of God in such a way that it "allows us to say that in him the Word that was the life of all things and the light of all human beings 'became flesh.'"[75] As Cobb explains, "It is not a matter of degree, but a different structure. It is not supernatural because there aren't just two structures, Jesus and everybody else."[76] As Cobb puts it, "we could say in the most literal sense that every fleshly entity enfleshes or "incarnates" God. But we can also make stronger claims about how God is present in Jesus."[77] In this way, Jesus shows forth a "qualitative and structural difference" because he is both revealed as the Christ, which is a personal identity that is both constitutively connected to the immanent *Logos* and also affects the future by instantiating his structure of existence in history and in particular the history of the church.[78] These metaphysical explorations of Christology have been enhanced in his recent work on Paul's letter to the Romans with David Lull. There he connects the revelatory and participatory effects of Jesus' life throughout the commentary as he works through Paul's use of *pistis*, which is often translated faith. The argument itself is impressive, but the concluding reflection on Romans 1:16-17 will demonstrate how Cobb's Process perspective can breathe in Pauline skin:

> We interpret Paul's statements in Romans 1:16-17 as pointing to the participation of believers in Jesus' faithfulness, which involves a real change in those who were bound to sin. Jesus' faithfulness breaks the bonds of sin for those who participate in Jesus' faithfulness, not sin. Anyone who participates in Jesus' faithfulness lives in the sphere of influence of that faithfulness, instead of in the sphere of sin's power. That does not mean they are no longer in danger of coming again under the bonds of sin, but it does mean that they can turn to the faithfulness of Jesus to deal with that danger.[79]

---

75. Ibid., 146-47.
76. Cobb, conversation with author, December 2, 2009.
77. Cobb, *Theological Reminiscences*, 282.
78. Cobb, "Jesus and Christ in Process Perspective," 145. See also Cobb, *Christ in a Pluralistic Age*, 138-43.
79. John B. Cobb Jr. & David Lull, *Romans* (St. Louis, MO: Chalice, 2005), 38. For a more developed explanation of the sphere of Jesus' influence in Romans, see Cobb and Lull, *Romans*, 116-20.

Paul may not be a Process theologian, but Cobb is clearly invested in establishing strong connections between his own project and the Christian tradition at large. This desire is not always shared or intentionally attended to by other Process thinkers, but it aids in contrasting his own work with that of Tanner.

Staging the Incarnation

One of the primary contrasts between *Logos* and Spirit Christologies is the number of stages. As previously discussed, a Spirit Christology has traditionally identified Jesus as the Christ as something that emerges through the course of his life and is fully established by his resurrection. In contrast, *Logos* Christologies share a general 3-stage movement. They start in the beginning with a pre-existent Word or Wisdom that was present prior to God's decision to create. The second stage is the descent of the Word into the world, with this descent completing itself either in the incarnation as seen in John's prologue, or in Jesus' death on a cross as seen in the Christ hymn of Philippians. The final stage is the resurrection of Jesus and his ascension to his rightful place in the divine life. This narrative is the skeletal outline of a familiar account of salvation history. For much of church history, the church's own self-understanding of its history corresponded to its salvation history, in which the coming of the Word in Christ was the both the center and revelation to the world of its coming future. To benefit from the dialogue between Tanner and Cobb, the challenges to this salvation history must be acknowledged.

When the church came to be the dominant arbiter of power across the West and the non-Christian other's difference was safely tucked away into Christendom's missiological goals, salvation history became both an unconscious meta-narrative and normative for theological reflection. It was not until the church's unity fractured that the story came under self-examination again. The challenges began to build, each one unraveling another string of Christendom's naiveté. First came the battles for the true church that emerged with the Protestant Reformation and then came the shock of an entirely autonomous narrative of history with the scientific revolution. Today there is no safe harbor where one can safely repeat the story of salvation history and not be under threat. It is undeniable that our collective understanding of universal history is constantly being improved through the sciences, and given our growing awareness of religious pluralism and the emergence of a genuine secular mode of human existence, should one be emboldened enough to tell a salvation history, it must be with a much more humble tongue. Strikingly, today's Christian account of salvation history will more readily be located in a number of other crowded histories, such as the history of world religion, especially as located within living spiritual traditions or monotheistic religions. It is here, in the confluence of histories, that I want to engage both Tanner and Cobb.

As developed above, Tanner's Christology is clearly a contemporary account of salvation history, and yet she is not blindly reasserting the tradition. She rather puts significant effort into describing the nature of theological reflection and its connection to the world. Having examined Cobb's process philosophy, we will turn toward Tanner's account of Christian talk about God and creation. As in Cobb's thought, Tanner sees a significant overlap between her Christology and her doctrine of Creation, including the problem of evil.[80] For Tanner, it is the radical transcendence of God that makes possible God's imminence in Creation. In the text that came out of her dissertation, God and Creation, she develops a theological methodology which she has continued to use throughout her career. There she points toward two significant contradictions latent in Christian talk about Creation, namely the tension between God's transcendence and imminence and the tension between God's absolute sovereignty and human freedom.[81] As she understands the theologian's job, the task is to show how the first-order theological language that comes from the life of the community of faith can be developed into a cohesive second-order account. This process she terms "transcendental deduction."[82] When it comes to tackling these two explicit tensions in the relationship between God and Creation she articulates two principles: "a non- competitive relation between creatures and God, and second, a radical

---

80. Kathryn Tanner, "Is God in Charge?" in *Essentials of Christian Theology*, ed. William C. Placher (Louisville, KY: Westminster John Knox, 2003), 121-22.
81. Kathryn Tanner, *God and Creation in Christian Theology: Tyranny or Empowerment* (Minneapolis, MN: Fortress, 2005), 19, 37-38.
82. Hughes, "'Tehomic' Christology," 260-61.

interpretation of divine transcendence."[83] Tanner's understanding of transcendence is akin to Barth in its intensity. She rejects any metaphysical account in which God is part of a system or a supreme being, by insisting that God is "beyond kinds" so much so that the ontological distinction between the Creator and the creatures is impenetrable.[84] Because of the radical transcendence of God, Tanner can understand divine immanence in a non-competitive way, making transcendence the necessary condition for genuine immanence. The tensions between God's transcendence and immanence or God's sovereignty and freedom are paradoxical and problematic since the question concerned the creaturely plane. In Tanner's mind, God resists the seemingly first-order theological predicaments by transcending them. For example, from a creaturely perspective, humans cannot have genuine freedom while God remains completely sovereign. And yet, because God is radically transcendent, God is not a cause among other causes, which would problematize the assumptions latent in the tension itself. Tanner sees the ontological distinction between Creator and creatures to be a nameless distinction because it resists any linguistic attempt to draw the necessary distinctions which make predication of God possible.[85] For this reason, Tanner "pictures the whole world, in all its complexity of causal process, as a horizontal place, suspended into existence at each and every point, by the vertical threads (invisible and infinitesimal) of God's own working."[86] Yes, the radicalism of God's transcendence is supposed to support structurally a ubiquitous connection with all the immanent plane, but the picture of vertical threads is disconcerting for an Open and Relational theologian.[87] While Tanner insists that these vertical strings do not threaten the integrity of the creaturely connections and relationships, it raises the problem of evil in a significant way.

The questions of evil and the incarnation are related here in Tanner, as they were in different ways in Cobb. As Hughes points out, since "Tanner is unable to identify God's agency any more with the unfolding of justice than with the perpetration of evil," both the character of God is in jeopardy, along

---

83. Tanner, *Jesus, Humanity and the Trinity*, 2-3. See also Tanner, *God and Creation*, 46-47 and Tanner, "Is God in Charge?" 120, 128.

84. Tanner, "Is God in Charge?" 119-120.

85. Tanner, *God and Creation*, 46.

86. Tanner, "Is God in Charge?" 129.

87. Hughes, "'Tehomic' Christology," 262.

with God's ability to take sides in history with the poor and oppressed.[88] The closest Tanner gets to addressing this question is in a footnote in which she states that, "it is axiomatic that God creates only what is good" and therefore, "questions of sin and evil are left out" of her account of God and Creation.[89] For the incarnation in particular, Tanner insists that the relationship of Jesus' divinity and humanity shows forth that the transcendence of God means that "everything with a human cause also has a divine cause," making the incarnation as much a paradox of Creation as Christology.[90] The singularity of Jesus is therefore not a causal reality, for every reality has a non-competitive divine and creaturely cause. The subjectivity of Jesus is then paradoxically incidental to his sonship. The sonship of Christ is not inclusive of anyone else, and therefore any other creaturely connection to the Father is derivative of this eternal relation.[91] Tanner states it with clarity when she says that, "because Christ's humanity is the pathway by which we receive the Spirit, his humanity must be fully transformed by the Spirit to give it, fully filled up with the Spirit in order for it to spill out and over to others."[92] Given both the exclusivity of God's goodness in Creation and the divinity of Jesus in the incarnation, one wonders if the non-competitive account that Tanner is hoping to articulate ultimately resolves the perceived contradictions she began with. Setting her account of the incarnation in her larger theological proposal sets the table for contrasting it with Cobb's.

Divine Initiative and Promise

While Cobb and Tanner have some significant foundational disagreements, there are several overlapping interests. For example, they both understand the incarnation to be a doctrine intimately connected to the doctrine of Creation and thus as primarily about God's self-investment in the world. Tanner's account of the nature of self-investment takes shape in her central theological thesis,

---

88. Ibid.
89. Tanner, *God and Creation*, 174n12.
90. Tanner, *Jesus, Humanity and the Trinity*, 21.
91. 274 Tanner, *Christ the Key*, 151.
92. Ibid., 171. See also Tanner, *Jesus, Humanity and the Trinity*, 11: "God is not simply opposed to the characteristics of human beings but beyond any such contrasts. It is that very radical transcendence that enables incarnation with what is other than God…Rather than coming at the expense of divinity, incarnation is the very thing that proves divinity."

namely that God desires to give Godself to Creation. The divine initiative and the story of salvation history that she articulates is structured so that through the incarnation, strong participation in the divine life is given as pure gift. The incarnation is then both revelatory of God's nature and grace, as well as the means by which Creation comes to participate in God. When set alongside Cobb's work, what is striking is how parallel certain affirmations are. Cobb begins with a natural theology, rejecting the radical transcendence that determines much of Tanner's work, and yet for Cobb, his metaphysical proposal is such that in each moment of becoming God both fully participates in the world and gives the gift of possibility. God feels with the world, judges and redeems what the world has become, and then gives to the world the gift and grace of new possibilities. Moment to moment, the luring insistence of God is offered to the world and the fullness of its becoming is received into God. This relationship is very much a non-competitive one, but it is sustained by the radical immanence that his di-polar account provides.

One reason that Tanner and Cobb are oddly sharing similar intuitions about divine initiative is that they both reject the typical framing distinction when considering the incarnation—namely the material versus the spiritual. This dualistic set-up is problematic to both Tanner and Cobb because of just what the incarnation reveals about the God-world relationship. For Tanner, creation out of nothing establishes the ontological distinction between Creator and creatures, fixing the grace-filled dignity of weak participation. Though humans are structurally more conscious of this reality, bearing the marks of God in their image-bearing constitution, all finite reality participates in God. This is a work of grace. Cobb also rejects a dualism of spirit and matter as a similar distinction that shapes his account of the world and the incarnation. For both, to be a creature is to have an existence and dignity flowing from God's initiative and work. The over-13-billion-year process which preceded the emergence of human beings is nothing less than the fruit of God's own ceaseless relationship with the world. To describe the world as a spiritually vacuous collection of matter is an impossibility for Cobb, for there is neither a world without God nor God without a world. The cosmic story of emergence is a universal story, but for Cobb, this natural story is a story of both God and the world. Just as all Creation shares in the dignity of weak participation as established in Tanner's depiction of Creation and thoroughly exemplified in her Christology, so too does the process understanding of subjectivity extend to all the world as exemplified in Jesus Christ. When, as Cobb describes, the initial aim of God co-constitutes the very self-hood of Jesus, we then see the enfleshment and extension of each moment's graceful gift of God, which is both the emergence of a new form of participation and a revelation of God's own primordial nature. Through Jesus' fidelity to the one he called *Abba*, he thus became the image of the invisible God.

Here an additional pair of parallel concepts come to the fore: their ideas about human nature and salvation. Tanner understands grace primarily as an expansion of our nature as image-bearers of God, being opened and connected through our weak participation. The incarnation brings salvation by being the perfect enactment of the capacities present through our weak participation. Here Tanner could hardly be more distanced from Cobb, for she insists that human nature cannot actualize these possibilities and that the possibilities themselves result from a grace which was gifted in the act of Creation. Goodness is not a possibility inherent in humanity, but one that only becomes possible because one adheres to God in Christ. Humans have to be given both God and themselves; and in doing so, grace comes to separate humanity from its nature, which is unity to God. Salvation, for Tanner, is a disjunctive leap. Through the eternal Son, human nature is transformed, but this transformation for full participation in the divine life is a rupturous event that originates in God alone. The ontological gap between the Creator and creatures is such that apart from God's free loving initiative there would be no connection to God. Underneath this depiction of the incarnation is Tanner's insistence on affirming both the total depravity of human nature and our identity as image bearers of God. The human predicament then has two features. First, the need for our sinful context to be changed, giving us a new community in which to understand our identities. And second, there is a need for a new nature capable of receiving the gift of the divine life as it participates in God. Her solution is the hypostatic union. This is "what Christians want to say" when they confess that Jesus Christ was both fully God and fully human. The incarnation is the means by which salvation by transformation of human nature takes place. The incarnation is not the product of pedagogical assent, cumulative inspiration, or the necessary preparation for the atoning work of the cross. The incarnation is the means by which God does for us what we could not do for ourselves—namely fit us and give us a share in the divine life. Given her anthropological picture, the hypostatic union represents the necessary articulation of God's divine initiative and self-investment in creation.

For Cobb, the hypostatic union is not the solution nor the doctrine that captures the nature of God's initiative and investment in the incarnation. The hypostatic union solved a philosophical problem that emerged from an experiential reality that is no longer needed. Articulating the same experiential reality with a process philosophy creates several initial contrasts with Tanner—namely that the incarnation is not a disjunctive event. The continuity between creation and the incarnation in Tanner is the grace of weak participation. Cobb's natural theology is such that the ontological gap between God and the world is eliminated, making the incarnation the fruit of God's initiative and investment in the world. Cobb's relational vision reorganizes how both the transformation of the individual's social context and new human nature are understood. Both features are much more organic emergent realities for Cobb. Early in his career, Cobb developed what he called the "structure of Christian existence" as a descriptive account of the experiential shape to Christian living in contrast to other great ways of being. Cobb recognized that the life of the Christian post-Easter continued to be shaped by Jesus Christ through the Spirit in which the radical demand of obedience to God was set in the context of God's love and initiative. Cobb argued that the structure of Christian existence was one in which we know ourselves as known and loved by God. In this existential experience of God's love, the person of faith can take responsibility for his life, and in doing so come to participate in the faithfulness of Jesus. Later in his career, Cobb connected this concept of the structure of Christian existence to the reign of God in the ministry of Jesus and the life of the Spirit in the early church, and has argued for the need to resist depersonalizing the language that Christians use for God to preserve the particular shape of Christian existence.

The Word of Creation and Word for Salvation

Over the course of this chapter, we have seen two distinct *Logos* Christologies. The featured contrast to explore here is the relationship between salvation history and universal history. Tanner gives a robust account of salvation history in which the God of grace both creates the conditions for and realizes creaturely participation in the divine life through the incarnation. It is the free loving initiative of God that acted to bring creation into being and into the divine life. Her nuanced anthropology facilitated a careful account of how salvation brought about a transformation of both the communal context and the individual's nature. While Tanner's description is evocative and the depiction of divine participation is alluring, for an open and relational theologian, the ontological gap between Creator and Creature is uncomfortable and her proposed "transcendental deduction" as a solution to the paradox of God's absolute sovereignty and human freedom is found to be unviable. The distance she creates between theological language and the world in which we live resists many key assertions that open and relational theologians make. Besides the tensions discussed above, in an essay on eschatology, she argues that if we can use the theological language of beginnings without there being a genuine beginning, we can likewise do so for eschatology. Interestingly, Tanner's observations about the relationship of science to constructive eschatology is revealing when it comes to her implied metaphysics. She observes, "if the scientists are right, the world for which Christians hold out hope ultimately has no future… destruction is our world's end."[93] While this may or may not be the most persuasive scientific picture, the assumption is that the connection between theological language and scientific accounts is minimal, a kind of non-overlapping magisteria that protects and enables recapitulations of the Christian tradition. For open and relational theologians, this is the primary issue in critiquing Tanner's theological assertions.

Cobb's proposal, while attending to the intuitions of the Christological controversies, is thoroughly set within a narrative of universal history. In fact, his first major publication of Christological work came after his development of a process natural theology. If we assume that Cobb's project is a valid theological endeavor, the primary questions surround how the theological commitments that emerged from a particular historical community surrounding a particular historical figure are to be understood today. There are three different places in which the vibrant contrasting character of Tanner's work highlights the challenge of an open and relational Christology. First, there is the recognition that the *Logos* tradition has long been a place where the church has insisted that the salvific encounter with God in Christ was God's intention from

---

93. Tanner, "Eschatology Without a Future?" 222.

the act of creation. The God whose Word became flesh is a God who chose to be a God who was for us. Second, *Logos* Christologies not only highlight the tension between salvation and universal history but represent the very symbol of the early church first used to expand the confessional horizon of their faith. Should there be a robust open and relational account of this, the *Logos* must not only connect these two narratives, but resist the temptation to relativize and supersede the tradition and history of Israel. Third, both Tanner and Cobb reject a dualistic narrative backdrop for a *Logos* Christology. The distinction between matter and spirit does not and should not determine the trajectory. Instead, as they both insist, the incarnation of the *Logos* need not be a divine invasion into the world but set in a larger ongoing story of divine participation in, with, and for the world. An open and relational Christology should seek to preserve the dynamism of Tanner's account without losing the metaphysical register modeled in Cobb's theology.

5

SALVATION FROM THE CROSS TO CREATION

In this chapter, I intend to explore two different Christologies centered on God's work of salvation in and through Jesus Christ. The work of Christ often serves as the starting point for Christology in Protestantism. Here we will look at two different Protestants theologians who begin and expand their Christologies by tending to the nature of salvation. Over the course of the chapter, five key features to their work have purchase for an Open and Relational vision. First, they both reject a clear line of distinction between the justification of the sinner and the process of sanctification. Second, they both insist that there is not a contradiction in the character of God and that of Jesus, including accounts of the cross. Third, there is an expansion of the context of salvation to all Creation. Just as the ministry of Jesus must set the context for the cross, Creation should be the backdrop of salvation. Fourth, the question of salvation is not for the sinner alone, but the sinned against. This means there can be no single narrative of redemption outside the context of one's relatedness. Fifth, an account of salvation that is thoroughly relational cannot minimize the horizontal elements, which include social, structural, and ecological concerns.

Beyond these five key features lies an important question: who needs salvation? The Open and Relational theologian Andrew Sung Park gives one of the most dramatic answers to this question. He argues that God too needs salvation. The reasons will become clear below, but when set alongside Liberal Reformed theologian Douglas Ottati, the contrasts will become important for part of the larger constructive goal. If Christology has both an existential and metaphysical register, one's understanding of salvation should shape one's doctrine of God. Park thus gives a dramatic picture of just what that could look like, but before we get there, we must first look at Ottati.

A Liberal Protestant's Christology of the Heart

Douglas Ottati is a liberal Protestants theologian for whom the liberal theological tradition remains vibrantly alive. More specifically, he is an Augustinian, Reformed, and liberal theologian who develops out of this location a theistic humanism, which he argues centers in the reconciling ministry and message of Jesus.[1] Early in his career, he published his first Christology: *Jesus Christ and Christian Vision: A Christology of the Heart*, in which he sought to describe the purpose and development of Christology as primarily the situated articulation of a particular piety that arose from the church's encounter and living experience of God in Christ. By highlighting the practicing and confessing communal shape of the theological story, Ottati brought to the fore what Jesus the first century Jewish Prophet, said, did, and endured as they pertained to these experiences. One should not be surprised that an heir of Schleiermacher and Edwards would turn his theological attention away from metaphysical speculation to heart-felt affection, but for Ottati our current historical situation calls for a more humble and open-handed confession grounded in the historical person of Jesus. While he does not insist on building his Christology upon the footnotes of historical Jesus scholars, a maneuver he problematizes beyond simply the historian's lack of consensus, he sees the Reformer's emphasis on Jesus' historical particularity as a guide.[2] The liberal theologians of the 19th century who prioritized the Christian's experience of Christ and the shape of life it brought forth, provide Ottati the trajectory from which he returns to the heart of Christology. For Ottati, Christology is primarily about God's work of redemption in Christ and not an explanation of his person. Thus, the tradition's testimony about his person results from the church's encounter with God through Christ, in and through the life of Jesus, which he sees as "an originating pattern for the Christian community's orientation in and perspective on the world" emerged.[3]

Before looking at several specific elements in Ottati's Christology, some general observations are necessary. First, for Ottati the shift from Christology

---

1. Douglas F. Ottati, *Theology for Liberal Protestants: God the Creator* (Grand Rapids, MI: Eerdmans, 2013), 19.
2. Douglas F. Ottati, *Jesus Christ and Christian Vision* (Louisville, KY: Westminster John Knox, 1996), 40.
3. Ibid., xi.

as a proposition to piety is part of his larger theological method, which, akin to Schleiermacher, understands Christianity as a particular tradition within a larger account of religion. It is beyond the purpose of this enquiry to assess it, but understanding how it functions is necessary to grasp the specificity of his Christology. Second, Ottati's theistic humanism is grounded in a radical monotheistic account of Christianity. This means that his appropriation of the Reformed tradition is thoroughly theocentric and his account of God as Creator is determinative for his account of God as Redeemer. Third, he sees Christian self-understanding as inseparable from the person of Jesus. For Ottati, the revelatory nature of the Christ event has two elements which must be accounted for—its contingency and universality. As dual elements of a piety for a specific community, the tension between these two takes a unique shape. For many, redemption can have a rather narrowed focus, looking at the relationship between God and the individual, yet when nested in the larger framework of creation, it need not narrow the event to an individualistic, tribal, or even anthropocentric horizon.

The Creator is the Redeemer

Ottati describes the current historical age as one of dislocation.[4] By dislocation, he means something more specific than a dislocation from the perceived security one had in a world with a shared sacred canopy. What Ottati emphasizes is that by breaking the link from the great chain of being, we not only moved beyond the settled hierarchy of the cosmos that dominated in Christendom, but we also ended up dislocated from each other, the world, and even ourselves. The question that motivates Ottati is primarily one of Creation
— "what is the place and worth of human beings?"[5] At the heart of the Biblical witness, Ottati sees a strong affirmation of Creation. All the cosmos and its diversity of creatures, including humanity, are primarily related to and valued by its Creator. All Creation is interconnected and those who are conscious of these connections are called to be both responsible in their living and in awe of its grandeur. This is what Ottati calls theistic humanism. It is a theocentric

---

4. Ottati, *Theology for Liberal Protestants,* 17.
5. Ibid.

humanism because God's role as Creator gives dignity to all creatures and to the story of its history.[6]

If our age of dislocation has led to human beings living lives shaped first by their own desires, impoverished relations, and lack of meaning, Ottati insists that we must understand the redeeming God in Christ first as the Creator of all. The Christian faith, along with the other monotheistic traditions, has inherited a Creation piety, and today this needs to be retrieved, expanded, and cultivated as the framework for faithful living and receiving the gift of Christ. We must expand creation piety to locate humanity in the constantly expanding awareness of the cosmos and the interplay of relationships between the Creator and all of Creation. In describing this Creation piety, Ottati emphasizes how it displaces but also repositions human beings within Creation, before God, and toward all living neighbors.[7]

The affirmation of God as Creator is not, for Ottati, a proposition to be settled by science. In fact, for Ottati the transcendence of God is such that God could never be objectively deduced to be the Creator, for God is not an object. God made the world, but the world becomes Creation when one's heart is attuned to it. Creation is not an affirmation to be defended, but a directive of one's piety. Here he echoes H. Richard Niebuhr's distinction between inner and outer history, such that the outer element of the world is the object studied and examined.[8] The inner element experiences the world in a participatory sense and there encounters something deeper, but not alien to the world—the world known as Creation. As Ottati puts it, "religious persons and communities take certain emotions, sensibilities, and affections to point not only toward more immediate objects and others that push back but also to an additional felt dimension, background, presence, order, matrix, or pattern that impinges on them."[9] This is essential for grasping the coterminous presence of the sovereign Creator to Creation. God is never experienced as another object within Creation, but as a "peculiar Object" or "Other" present to and through Creation. This means that religious affections and emotions are not expressions of subjectivity but are real encounters with an object—namely God. A

---

6. Ibid., 18.
7. Ibid., 122.
8. H. Richard Niebuhr, *The Meaning of Revelation* (Louisville, KY: Westminster John Knox, 2006), 56-60, 84-85.
9. Ottati, *Theology for Liberal Protestants,* 45.

particular religious community will have its own cultural-linguistic infrastructure that shapes it, and yet Ottati insists that there is more than just this orientating factor. In monotheistic traditions, one is oriented toward the good God of Creation.[10] In Christianity, through Christ, we come to see that the one who redeems is the one who creates all things and holds all things in God's power, for the Redeemer is the Creator. This also means that the Redeemer is concerned about nothing less than the whole of Creation, for the Creator is the Redeemer of all things.

That the Redeemer is the Creator gives a kind of broad background or a compass for Ottati's understanding of redemption. Because the Creator is the Redeemer, Creation is not inert or relegated to the background of humanity's salvation story. In our cosmic perspective, we must decenter ourselves as a species and recognize that all Creation is on its way toward redemption and contained within certain vectors of grace, gift, and promise.[11] By holding these two things together, Ottati can capture that the wideness of God's mercy involves all of creation and that creation is so connected with redemption that grace and gift are both intrinsic to Creation.

By nesting redemption within his understanding of Creation, Ottati follows a specifically Reformed shape to theology. Like both Calvin and Schleiermacher, the doctrine of God and Christ are not dealt with in an explicitly full way up front but expands throughout his entire account of God's relationship to the world as Creator-Judge-Redeemer.[12] The identity of God is understood first through God's economic relations with the world. This is in part why he emphasizes the relationship between Creation and redemption. The context for understanding God's work in Christ is God's identity as Creator. There are two consequences for this worldly or Creation-nested form of Christianity. First, it means that the entire world belongs to God and is called to respond faithfully to God. God is not just present to all, but sovereign over all. There can be no proper division of the sacred from secular, the religious from the profane, or the material from the spiritual. God, the Creator and Judge, has a will for all Creation. Second, the theistic humanism advanced by Ottati rejects temptations toward utopian visions, ethical relativism, and demands for purity.

---

10. Ibid., 67.
11. Ibid., 249-54.
12. Ibid., 167-68.

This form of worldly Christianity offers what Ottati calls a "hopeful realism."[13] It simultaneously recognizes God's love, judgment, and dream for the world, while calling one to invest oneself in it. It is hopeful because the hope is in God the Creator who is also the Redeemer. It is realistic because it does not deny the contested and conflicted situation that the people of God find themselves in within history. The God of history is not alien to it and neither should God's people be.

If Creation sets the context for redemption, one can see how Ottati could develop a more robust Christology from below and from the heart. A strong theocentrism and Creation-piety are definitely categories one could take into account when assessing the person of Jesus. Before doing so, we must collect a few observations. First, whatever shape the account of redemption takes, it will include all Creation; going beyond an anthropocentric horizon to include the cosmos. Second, this expansion allows God's redemption to address the questions Ottati sees at the heart of the age of dislocation. Third, as a theocentric humanist, Ottati will resist any form of Christocentrism that narrows or places boundaries on God's good will. Fourth, when the concept of Creation is understood to give shape to a particular piety and affirm God's sovereign and universal presence, redemption must do the same. Fifth, to say that the Creator is the Redeemer is not to assert a connection held in God's identity, but to assert that the character of Creation, God's judgment, and redemption, all share in the grace and gift of God revealed in Christ. Said another way, the grace found through a redemptive encounter with Christ is also then revealed to be at the heart of Creation. Lastly, anticipating further reflection on the person of Jesus, God's redemption is a recapitulation of what was given at Creation.

The Revelatory Nature of the Christ Event

The problem with Christology, as Ottati describes it, is articulating "both the centrality and the particularity of Jesus Christ without being shackled by the problematic terms and conceptualities of the past."[14] Ottati is not antagonistic to the tradition but recognizes the tradition as itself living and responsible to the lived experience of Christ's body today. He emphasizes three primary reasons

---

13. Douglas F. Ottati, *Hopeful Realism Reclaiming the Poetry of Theology* (Eugene, OR: Wipf & Stock, 2009).
14. Ottati, *Jesus Christ and Moral Vision,* 20.

we need a new constructive account of Christology. First, he highlights the distance between the experience of faith and the dynamics of history from the metaphysical language of the councils. Second, the Gospels' actual depiction of Jesus is not that compatible with the traditional formulas and has had the effect of directing the church's attention away from the life of Jesus toward a metaphysical conclusion about it. Third, there is the difficulty of giving an adequate account of both Jesus' humanity and divinity given the terms of the tradition.[15] These concerns do not lead Ottati to throw Chalcedon into the waste heap of history. He argues that if the metaphysical conclusions were understood symbolically, fidelity to the tradition's intended insight needs to be redescribed. For Ottati, "the correctness of Chalcedon's symbolic intent to insist upon a profound mystery, namely that Jesus Christ is decisive for how we are to envision both God and human life appropriately related to God."[16] The historical development that led up to the Chalcedonian definition used metaphysical language for what Ottati identifies as the insistence upon the particularity and centrality of Christ. In moving beyond the metaphysical limitations of Hellenistic philosophy, Ottati argues that Christology must again begin with the particularity of Jesus—from below—for this figure remains the singular focus for the Christian vision of God and humanity's place in Creation.

One cannot simply begin with the Gospels when one turns to the particularity of Jesus. The Gospels, Ottati emphasizes, are already an evaluative form of literature. They reflect not simply the particular historical life of Jesus, but the continued experience of God he mediated in the life of the church. The Gospels construction and selection into canon was an act of the church and they presented four different portraits of what Jesus said, did, and endured. It is important for Ottati that the Gospels are not biographies nor histories. His interest is in what the cumulative affirmation and reception of the Gospels presents. To express what he intends to retrieve from the Gospels, he compares and contrasts his effort with Bultmann. He notes that Bultmann was right to argue that demythologizing the Gospels is nearly impossible, and that a path back to the historical Jesus cannot be established through them.[17] More than

---

15. Ibid., 39-42.
16. Ibid., 45.
17. Ibid., 51ff.

that, Bultmann rightly points the theologian beyond the goal of historical reconstruction and toward the kerygma of the Gospel. The kerygma is not something a historian can deduce, but is a "decisive revelation of God and a decisive possibility for human life in appropriate relation to God."[18] The problem Ottati highlights is that, for Bultmann, demythologizing ends up with little content left for informing the Christian and their living response to God. Ottati insists that historical engagement should not defang the person of Jesus in the Gospels from making a claim upon the lives of his disciples. Since only disciples call Jesus the Christ and disciples then and now tell and retell the story of Jesus, what is being communicated in the Gospels is not primarily history, but the character of Jesus' life lived before God and toward his neighbors. Historical insights can assist and direct our attention when engaging the Gospels, but it should not determine them. The heart of the Gospels and the heart of Christology is the life of Jesus—one lived with radical devotion to God.

Connecting the life of Jesus and his own piety to the one he called *Abba* to the life of his disciples is important for Ottati. His Christology of the heart is premised on his thesis that "human subjectivity comes to significant expression in patterns of behavior."[19] These patterns of behavior, while not fully conscious to anyone, are connected to their dispositions, affections, desires, and devotions.[20] Should one assess Jesus, or anyone for that matter, on a single action or from a single encounter, clarity is not possible. But when placed in narrative scope, the heart and mind of a person comes into view. It is here that Ottati sees the Gospels as revelatory of Jesus' particularity. In the Gospels, we see both consistent patterns of behavior and the directedness of his subjectivity. In this view, there is an integrity within the New Testament about the piety and practice of Jesus, one that was offered and extended in the Gospels to the disciples and even depicted in the letters Paul.[21] For Ottati, "the Gospels are narratives that are constructed to portray, among other things, an agent's inward

---

18. Ibid., 52.
19. Ibid., 55.
20. Ibid., 57.
21. Ottati here points to the Philippians 2 hymn as evidence when Paul gives a preface to the doxological account of Jesus' own piety saying, "Let the same mind be in you that was in Christ Jesus." Phil. 2:5 (NRSV). Ottati also argues in the forthcoming *A Theology for the Twenty-First Century* (Grand Rapids, MI: Eerdmans, forthcoming) that the resonance between the call Jesus put on his disciples and that of Paul to the churches he ministered to can be seen in charges such as, "live your life in a manner worthy of the gospel" Phil. 1:27 (NRSV).

affections in relation to externals, and so to reveal a character and recommend a way of living."[22] This means that the totality of the Gospel proclaimed the life of Jesus; and that what he said, did, and endured, are included in the Christological work.

The work of God in Christ is not communicable apart from the entire presentation of the life of Jesus. For Ottati, this emphasis may be broader than many Protestants who have focused intensely on the cross, but part of what the Chalcedonian insistence includes is this affirmation that God was present and being revealed in the fullness of Jesus' humanity. For the disciple then, the life of Jesus is both the model of living before God and the means by which one comes to share life in God. The key for Ottati is the recognition that one's connection to God is inseparable from the devotion in one's heart. Faith, especially faith in Christ, is not a series of metaphysical affirmations nor is it even a set of ethical prescriptions. Faith in Christ is foremost about where one directs one's love.

As it was for Jesus, the object of a disciple's affection is God. For Ottati, two primary virtues of Jesus demonstrate this. First is the monotheistic loyalty of Jesus to the one he called *Abba*. Second are Jesus' attentive care, love, and action for his neighbor. Of course, these two are intertwined, as they are in the Greatest Commandment, but for Ottati they represent the heart of Christology itself. In the life of Jesus, these elements combine for a patterned expression of his personality. When Jesus' emotional constitutions take the form of enacted love, they are not simply to be understood as responses to his neighbors and enemies, but also as responses that are shaped by his abiding loyalty and response to God. Jesus had radical devotion to God. A devotion that put all other things in their proper place and directed Jesus' own life and living. In this way, Ottati understands Jesus to be a revelation of a human fully devoted, faithful, loving, and living towards God. Yet in and through Jesus' radical fidelity, received in faith, Jesus is a revelation of a God who is fully devoted, faithful, loving, and living with us and for us.[23]

A Christology of the heart is one in which what Jesus said, did, and endured comes to shape the life of one who calls him the Christ. For the disciple, Jesus teaches, embodies, and empowers a way that reorients the devotions of

---

22. Ottati, *Jesus Christ and Moral Vision*, 65.
23. Ibid., 115.

our hearts—a reorientation in which our will is loosened from its own determination toward God. As Ottati puts it, "the main point is that the way that comes to us in Jesus Christ enlarges our hearts and our visions toward love of God and neighbor. Love of God and neighbor go together, since hearts and minds oriented toward God are no longer curved in upon self and self's private interest."[24] Here one can see how Jesus' monotheistic loyalty strongly echoes H. Richard Niebuhr's radical monotheism. For Niebuhr, polytheistic faiths are those which orient themselves towards many objects of meaning and value and henotheistic faiths are those that orient toward a closed group or society.[25] The radical monotheistic faith is oriented toward God alone. Yet, like the monotheistic loyalty of Jesus, in recognizing the idolatrous religious affections when one directs their love toward any finite reality, one also recognizes the divine affirmation and ethical call toward all finite things at the heart of radical monotheism. The heart of one given fully to God and God alone is one which will give themselves in love toward the world. In this way, one can see the Christological argument for Ottati's theocentric humanism. The rich depiction of Jesus Christ within the Gospels is one, "whose teaching both elicits and proclaims confidence in and loyalty to God as a dominant devotion that lends authentic orientation to human life in God's world."[26] For Jesus and the Disciple alike, the love of God the Creator of all is a love which directs us towards God's creatures and their well-being.

For Ottati, Jesus Christ discloses the reality of God and the purposes of God. When you look at Jesus, one thing you should see is a kind of demonstration, a disclosure of who God is and what God's will is. This is one sense in which Jesus Christ is a revelation of God. The second element Ottati wants to emphasize is that when you look at Jesus, you look at God's Word and Wisdom focused in a particular person able to disclose uniquely this Word and Wisdom because he acts in a way that reflects and expresses it all the time. Jesus is then both a disclosure of God's Word and Wisdom made present in reality and a truly responsive human life which expresses this same Word and Wisdom. Said another way, the revelation of God in Christ is of both who God is and

---

24. Ibid., 130.
25. H. Richard Niebuhr, *Radical Monotheism and Western Culture: With Supplementary Essays* (Louisville, KY: Westminster/John Knox, 1993), 24-25 and 38.
26. Ottati, *Jesus Christ and Moral Vision*, 76.

what God is up to, and what human beings truly are and what they ought to be up to. What Jesus said and did has a central role in this account of God's work in Christ, but Ottati does not leave it there, for what Jesus endured has a specific redemptive role to which we now turn.

The Transferable Nightmare of the Cross

What Jesus endured was not simply the cross. The cross was the end of Jesus' ministry and, for Ottati, differentiating the events of the passion from Jesus' own passion for God and God's kingdom has historically been devastating to the church's reflection on the cross. It has served as an accomplice to the radical individualism in late modern Protestantism and helped create a narrative vacuum from which to understand the cross. Taken in light of what Jesus said and did, the cross is the conclusion of Jesus' own radical fidelity to God. What Jesus endured, the suffering that concluded in the cross is for Ottati a conclusion that came about through a historical cooperation of both perverse religious and political powers and Jesus' decision to remain faithful to the God who came to judge those very powers. Jesus did not die to bear the wages of each individual's sin, but died because of sin, bearing the death sin brings as an innocent one. For Ottati, "Jesus' crucifixion is the great occasion of innocent suffering unto death that hangs over all the many occasions of innocent suffering that continue to be the wages of sin in our history."[27] The sins for which Jesus suffered were the sins of others and, as such, the death of Jesus on the cross becomes a lens through which Christians come to understand the destructive and death-dealing power of sin in our world today. The cross of Christ is the occasion for giving the right nightmares and revulsions.

As Ottati's sees it, the question of the cross that the church has long wrestled with is just how the crucifixion, a long and torturous death at the hands of enemies, can be a central part of the gospel message of grace and salvation. That the church has insisted that this event is the very place God reveals the possibility of grace and goodness is not an easy theological assertion to deal with. To do this, Ottati gives an account in which the crucifixion and the judgment it brings to bear are themselves expressions of grace. Christian theologians can no longer minimize the atrocities that fill our history. The cross

---

27. Ibid., 87.

of Christ, in its unjust suffering, must not be swallowed in the glory of the Resurrection, for as the cross-dead one, Jesus has many sisters and brothers.

The power of the cross, as itself a bearer of grace, includes with it the power to transform human hearts away from their self-concern with their own power, privilege, possessions, and prestige, and toward repentance and transformation. Ottati points to a number of places in which the church has used the passion of Jesus as a place to be disturbed toward repentance. Following Josiah Royce, he gives the example of Bach's *St. Matthew's Passion* in which the disciples at the Last Supper respond to Jesus' assertion that one of them would betray him by asking "Is it I?" This question is then picked up by the chorus that Bach calls "The Believers" as it concludes with, "Tis I, My sins betray thee, who dies to make me whole."[28] In this artistic portrayal of the cross, we see the story being made contemporaneous to the believer. The innocent suffering and death of Jesus becomes the place in which they recognize their own participation in the very power of sin that put Jesus to death. They also recognize in his death God's desire for their own well-being in the face of their ignorance. Ottati says, "The power made perfect in weakness is one that often inhabits the underside of history, but it persists as an undying protest against the insatiable desires of every oppressive agent."[29] When the cross becomes an expression of grace, it does so by disturbing and disclosing the believer's own participation in the death-dealing power of sin. The cross was not just a nightmare for Jesus or even the one he called *Abba*, but can and should be a transferable nightmare to all disciples.

Ottati develops three observations to expand his proposal. First is the recognition that the crucifixion of Jesus was a historical response by certain contemporaneous powers to his kingdom message and the way of life he embodied and to which he called others. In both his call to radical fidelity to God and his commitment to his neighbors, especially the least of these, his ministry was far from benign to the powers that be. Second, Ottati notes that individual actions are not committed in isolation, even if they originate from a single person's desires, for the social nature and connections of human beings are not something we can be abstracted from. More than that, a sinful act of any person originates from the sin that person participates in at a corporate level. As

---

28. Ibid., 87-88.
29. Ibid., 88.

Ottati states, "misdirection or construction of the heart—its loyalties, attitudes, purposes, intentions, and so on—has a personal basis in the complex and even conflicting aspects of human emotional constitution", and yet, in the background lies social structures which "work upon the emotional or affective constitutions of people."[30] Recognition of this structural and social role of sin, which we are all born into, means that sin has an objective power in the world.[31] Third, Ottati not only wants to recognize that the innocent continue to suffer like Jesus, but also insist that the suffering of the innocent both then and now is a demonstration of the reigning order of society. Those who die on crosses today do not simply have an analogical relationship to Jesus, but serve as a point of genuine disclosure, of a revealing of the objective power of sin in the world.

Part of what the crucifixion is meant to show is who exactly crucified Jesus; namely powers, principalities, and persons who reflect certain commitments. It is those commitments, acknowledged or hidden, that need to be changed. No Christian is off the hook for Ottati, because the element of grace present on the cross insists believers witnessed the crucifixion and betrayed the one who died to make us whole. That is the nightmare we are being given, and that nightmare addresses us in fundamental ways. The cross addresses us to change our hearts. It is a full-frontal assault on the wrong desires and the wrong loves that characterize our hearts.

The most powerful example he gives of just what the grace of the right nightmare looks like is the story of Scrooge from Charles Dickens' *Christmas Carol*.[32] Scrooge is literally an old man who will be made new. For Ottati, *Christmas Carol* is Charles Dickens' attempt to articulate, in his own terms, the meaning of Christianity and the power of the cross. This old man, being blessed with the right nightmares, is made new. And how it happens in the text is important. At the beginning of the story, some people show up and directly address the selfishness of Scrooge by giving him a direct call to compassion and generosity amidst the Christmas season. Scrooge is not moved and dismisses them and their ethical imperatives. Scrooge's heart is shown to have a mighty

---

30. Ibid., 89.

31. Ottati here quotes Schleiermacher's insight into the social nature of sin that "in each the work of all and in all the work of each." Ibid.

32. Ottati, *Theology for Liberal Protestants*, 84.

fortress that protects him from any recognition of his sin-sick soul and the suffering he is responsible for. The grace which Scrooge receives thus comes from his dead friend Marley, who worked out a last chance which becomes an occasion of grace for Scrooge. This occasion for grace is frightening visitations by spirits who show him his own life and certain possibilities. After being visited by the ghosts of the past, present, and future, the visions end with Scrooge falling on his own grave. Scrooge is graced with the right nightmares, which turn his heart toward another possibility. And when he awakens the next morning, he does just that. With shouts of joy in the streets, he becomes a participant in God's world in a new and more beautiful way. For Ottati, Dickens' novella captures the grace that one receives in being blessed with the right nightmare.

The cross is at the heart of the gospel stories in both their telling and retelling. Today, disciples can have their deepest orientations and convictions challenged when the cross discloses the wages of our sin borne by others. What is being addressed here is the heart of the disciple, the need to re-orient their love. By showing the horrifying implications and consequences of the disciple's current death-dealing commitments and activities, the disciple is put in the situation for the possibility of transformation. The gift of the right nightmare is a disclosure of grace.

From the Heart of the Disciple to the Heart of God

To engage and expand upon Ottati's Christology, I want to turn to Korean-American theologian Andrew Sung Park. He is an Open and Relational theologian who has dedicated multiple works to engaging the Asian concept of *Han* and the doctrine of sin to develop a triune understanding of the atonement. Before turning to look at Park's work itself, I want to layout four areas that I intend to develop constructively going forward. First, Park gives significant attention to incorporating and expanding feminist and liberationist critiques of sin as developed in the Augustinian and Reformed traditions. The particular way in which Park does this makes his work a fruitful companion to Ottati's focus on the heart by expanding the attention beyond hubris. Second, Park joins Ottati in emphasizing the need to use what Jesus said, did, and endured in any account of salvation. Park, however, wants to pause and ask: for whom? Here the concept of *Han* aids Park in identifying the people of *Han*; the victims, the sinned against, the underside, and the downtrodden who become themselves the answer to his question. Yes, the innocent suffering of Jesus can occasion nightmares for the violator, but what of the victims? More than that, what the totality of what Jesus said, did, and endured, communicates about the reconciliation of victim and violator is essential for Park to identify the gospel as good news. Third, there is a significant contrast between the non-metaphysical Christology of heart and Park's triune atonement, because for Ottati the horizon of salvation is the inner life of the believer and not that of God. While this contrast is large, the connection between the redemptive affectivity of Ottati and the divine affectivity within Park's triune account of atonement creates a generative connection. Last, for Park the transferable nightmare of the cross should be affirmed, but also expanded in light of the triune nature of the cross. Park's proposal insists also upon a transferable solidarity with the cross-dead Christ and a transferable promise with the cross-dead but resurrected Son.

The Gospels and *Han*

Park begins his understanding of the work of Jesus Christ by first attending to the gospels themselves. For much of Church history, the atonement theories that have been developed were divorced from the rich accounts of Jesus' own ministry. If one examines the gospels closely, they will notice that Jesus lived both among and as a marginalized person. Jesus shared their experience of oppression by political, social, and religious authorities, and opposed these powers directly, all the way to the cross. The message of the kingdom of God was a message not just of repentance for sinners, but a message of hope, affirmation, and solidarity for the downtrodden.[33] Park insists that the place from which to begin an interpretation of the cross should be the very narrative of Jesus' mission in the gospels, his mission for which he was anointed—"The Spirit of the Lord is upon me, because he has anointed me to bring good news to the poor. He has sent me to proclaim release to the captives and recovery of sight to the blind, to let the oppressed go free, to proclaim the year of the Lord's

---

33. Park regularly appropriates a number of New Testament scholars including John Dominic Crossan, Richard Horsley, John Meier, and Walter Wink. For the purposes of this project the specific reconstruction of the historical Jesus will not be assessed in its detail but assumed for the purposes of comparing theological constructions.

favor..."[34] This picture of Jesus' ministry and death, for Park, is best understood through the Korean concept of *Han*.

Han, he notes, is not a concept easy to translate. In an earlier work, Park gives five different definitions including frustrated hope, the collapsed feeling of pain, the letting go of one's center, resentful bitterness, and the wounded heart.[35] Elsewhere, he describes *Han* as similar to a black hole in which a "victim's pain expands beyond his or her capacity for perseverance and the soul collapses into a deep and dark abyss. That abysmal core of pain is *Han,* and the collapsed inner core swallows everything, dominating the victim's life-agenda."[36] Here one can see that *Han* is not simply any particular wound, but also the power a wound comes to have when it draws the life out of the person and into the pit of their pain. *Han* is a festering wound that breeds bitterness, resignation, helplessness, and disengagement from life.

Important for Park is the recognition that *Han* operates at multiple levels, individual, collective, and structural, and that *Han* has a cyclical relationship with sin. At an individual level, *Han* can be seen in victims of abuse who are given over to their status as one who has been trampled on without dignity and self-respect. This situation, while being individual, can easily be understood to operate at multiple levels. For example, a situation of domestic abuse can have multiple other connections. At a collective level, in both conscious and unconscious ways, individuals may be victims of economic oppression, carry feelings of cultural inferiority, and feel helpless to imagine a life otherwise. At the structural level, Park identifies three main spirits at work which solidify themselves in the systems and institutions of the world—capitalism, sexism, and racism.[37] Connecting the three levels allows Park to give an account of *Han* and the human predicament that recognizes complexity of *Han*-ridden people and the inability to redress it apart from larger social and cultural transformations. This is important because too often the theological solution of a situation is directed toward the sinner and not the sinned against and is about forgiveness for an action and not the healing of a wound. By taking the deep

---

34. Luke 4:18-19 (NRSV).
35. Andrew Sung Park, *The Wounded Heart of God: The Asian Concept of Han and the Christian Doctrine of Sin* (Nashville, TN: Abingdon, 1994), 15-30.
36. Andrew Sung Park, "The God Who Needs Our Salvation," in *The Changing Face of God*, ed. Frederick W. Schmidt (New York: Thomas More, 2000), 82.
37. Park, *The Wounded Heart of God*, 67.

wounds seriously, the multiple levels of *Han* must all be addressed, and we must understand the problem of sin in its complex and cyclical relationship with *Han*. Sin can cause *Han* and over time, *Han* comes to cause sin. As a cycle, this can lead to "an intractable and darker state of affairs that may be called evil."[38] Because Christian theology has been so concerned with sin to the exclusion of *Han*, our understanding of the work of God in Christ has primarily been about sinners and not their victims. This has meant that the neglected, violated, and suffering object has been ignored for the acting subject. As Park puts it, "in this one-sided scheme, it seems everything, including God, exists for the well-being of the subject. Victims are the objects whose salvation is outside the concern of the subject."[39] For Park this demands a revolution in the doctrine of sin and salvation, and yet one needs to look no further than the Gospels themselves to see one.

The Gospels tell a good news story for the *Han*-ridden people. Park emphasizes how Jesus practiced deep solidarity with the victims of his time, noting that apart from a robust recognition of this connection, one can easily misunderstand the cross. Park highlights four elements to Jesus' solidarity: sharing a common goal, a communal identity, commiseration, and liberative world.[40] First, Jesus established solidarity with victims as the central purpose of his mission at his inaugural sermon in Luke 4. Jesus not only preached the liberation of oppression, but taught, lived, and called others into a community around this mission. In fact, in Luke-Acts, Jesus anoints and sends the disciples out to do this mission twice in his ministry. Then after his resurrection, but before his ascension Jesus teaches them about the kingdom of God for forty days and tells them that once the same spirit that came upon him comes to them they are to do the same. If the same community on a kingdom mission is being sent before and after the resurrection, this missional solidarity was and should be at the heart of understanding the work of God in Christ. Second, Jesus himself identified with the downtrodden. In one sense, he was a marginalized Jew in the first century so this should not come as a surprise, but more than that in his teaching Jesus regularly told parables where God identified with the

---

38. Park, "The God Who Needs Our Salvation," 83.
39. Park, *The Wounded Heart of God*, 73.
40. Andrew Sung Park, *Triune Atonement: Christ's Healing for Sinners, Victims, and the Whole Creation* (Louisville, KY: Westminster John Knox, 2009), 42.

marginalized. Perhaps the most impressionable example is the parable of the last judgement in Matthew in which Jesus states his own identity was with the least of these.[41] Third, Jesus commiserated with the marginalized in a very specific way, by bearing their *Han*. For Park, this element cannot be understated for understanding the cross. Echoing the Gospel of Matthew 8:17, he notes that "he has borne not our sin or our iniquity, but our infirmities and diseases—*han*."[42] The commiseration with the downtrodden means that Jesus not only knows the experience of agony, pain, sorrow, and the struggle they live with, but also has become their friend, advocate, and liberator there, in the struggle. Isolating this lifelong identification with the downtrodden from theological reflection on the cross is costly.

The fourth feature of Jesus' solidarity with the victims is his enactment of liberation. The ministry of Jesus addressed the specific cultural, physical, social, and religious forms of disease, oppression, and suffering. In many ways, the ministry of Jesus included a frontal assault on the principalities and powers that diminished the lives of many he encountered.[43] It was not simply that people were being liberated, but that this liberation was itself an enactment of his mission. As Park rightly emphasizes, the healing and deliverance Jesus brought involved resolving their *Han*. He contrasts healing versus curing to bring this distinction to the fore. Resolving a particular problem is a cure, but restoring a person physically, socially, mentally, and spiritually is a genuine healing. What the healing ministry of Jesus demonstrates then is a solidarity with the victims that goes from problem solving to problem sharing and transforming. The solidarity to the *Han*-ridden people Jesus embodied is not his alone, but God's. For Park, a proper account of the cross and resurrection needs to be set in this context, namely that in Christ, God has fully identified with the *Han*-ridden people, even to death on a cross such that they too may share in his liberation from death.

The Cross in the Heart of God

The above discussion surrounding Park's understanding of Jesus' ministry to the *Han*-ridden is important for this chapter, but it should also be noted that his

41. Matthew 25:31-46 (NRSV).
42. Park, *Triune Atonement*, 43.
43. Ibid., 44.

account of Jesus' ministry also deals, like Ottati's, with the challenge Jesus' ministry puts to the powerful.[44] For this chapter we need to turn to his account of the cross and resurrection in the life of God and ultimately his triune rendering of the work of Christ.

As an Open and Relational theologian, Park argues that through the solidarity of Jesus with the *Han*-ridden people, God also comes to share and participate in *Han*. Even stronger than that, he states that the very "paradox of the Jesus-event" is this, "the invulnerable God became vulnerable in Christ."[45] By insisting that God is revealing Godself in the life, ministry, death, and resurrection of Jesus, Park argues that God too shares in the experience of the *Han*-ridden people. God's perfect love, imaged in Christ, is a love that participates in such a way that God is not invulnerable to *Han*, but knows it within the divine life itself. "The cross of Jesus nakedly exposes the woundedness of God. It is not only the symbol of God's effort to save humanity but also the symbol of God's inexpressible *Han* shared with other victims. Our sin-offended and *Han*-suffering God is crying out for justice and healing."[46] God too is *Han*-ridden, because God has chosen to share life with the victims of this world. The cross then becomes a historical eruption of God's *Han* in history. On the cross of Christ, the oppressed discover a God who suffers with them, because God is for them. From the perspective of the oppressors, the cross of Christ can also occasion a divine recognition—namely that God suffers at their hands. This means that there is a cross in the heart of God and on the cross, we see God's *Han*.

Park is aware of the consequences for arguing that God too is a *Han*-ridden victim. He is clear that this means the work of salvation is no longer something creatures alone need, for God also needs salvation. This could at first seem like a strong statement. Once the relational nature of genuine salvation is recognized, one that realizes that sin and *Han* cannot be dealt with in any final away in isolation, saying God needs us for salvation is akin to saying God has

---

44. Park gives a powerful argument for preserving the symbolic use of Jesus' blood. For the oppressed the blood of Jesus is a symbolic testimony toward God's participation in their suffering and for the oppressors it remains a constant protest of God against all powers that unjustly spill blood today. As Park puts it, "Jesus' blood as a symbol - organic and living - represents the collective voice of numerous victims crying out for justice and truth." See Park, *Triune Atonement*, 35-36.

45. Park, "The God Who Needs Our Salvation," 84.

46. Ibid., 89.

chosen, through God's own self-investment in the world to not be God without Creation. In Christ, God reveals that the God who is love has not just created a world out of love and for loving relation with God, but has also been so moved by Creation as to open God's own life to Creation. God's salvation and the salvation of Creation are linked. In Christ, we see that God is a cross-bearing God and not a cross-building one. Salvation then cannot be accomplished by negating this divine determination and thus must embrace a contradictory form of power.

The reciprocal nature of salvation points towards three key insights for Park. First, God did not need to spill Jesus' blood to forgive the sin of the world. When sin is understood apart from *Han*, the cross easily becomes the means by which sin is conquered. But for Park, God does not need one more sacrifice (even a divine one) to forgive. Park states, "If God cannot forgive sinners without the violent execution of Jesus, God is neither gracious nor merciful, but interested only in retributive justice."[47] Jesus died because of the violence of sinners, a violence that Creation is still groaning over. Second, this means that God's presence and participation in the world through the life of Jesus was both a risk and binding for God. It was a risk in that God was truly vulnerable to the very experiences of suffering and injustice that too many share. The cross not only exposed and revealed God's broken-heartedness and wounded-ness, but Godself was exposed on the cross, generating *Han* within the divine life itself. In this way, the risk turns into a binding in which God too is sin-injured and *Han*-suffering. For Park, God in God's own self needs salvation and healing, and this cannot be done outside of relationship with Creation.

Last, the reciprocal nature of salvation necessitates a re-envisioning of divine power. In the face of evil and suffering, God reveals God's strength through endurance. God's experience as a victim is not a reason for Park to deny the power of God, but it recognizes that divine power is in part the upside-down power of the cross. The weakness of God is power, for God is strong enough to embrace the violence of sin and still forgive it and work towards healing. The compassion of God defines God's power. To the abused and downtrodden, the cross speaks a powerful word of solidarity, and to the perpetrator, the cross protests against abusive power and unjust suffering.

---

47. Andrew Sung Park, *From Hurt to Healing: A Theology of the Wounded* (Nashville, TN: Abingdon, 2004), 27.

For Park, God's nature and name as the God of love is on the line throughout history. Because the cross is the eruption of God's *Han* in history, the character of the divine essence itself is inseparable from the future, and especially the promise of the resurrection.[48] The resurrection of the cross-dead Jesus is necessary for salvation. In fact, the resurrection understood from the perspective of the *Han*-ridden people is not simply about the future of Jesus. Just as God had great solidarity with people through the life and death of Jesus, so too does the resurrection of Jesus expand this solidarity. The resurrection of Jesus from the dead into the life of God is a promise that all those who die on crosses have a future in God. The resurrection of Jesus is the first fruits of this promise, and so we live in hope. However, this hope is not simply for the sinned against, but for sinners too. Likewise, this hope is not primarily about being reconciled to God alone, but also about being reconciled one to another before God as well. Recognizing its relational nature, Park defines salvation by stating that it is "not a type of state, but the quality of the intensity of divine presence in relationships."[49] Salvation is not something one can attain, but something one lives into.[50] In order for salvation to emerge for God, victim, and violator alike, the promise of the resurrection is necessary. Not only does creation groan and humanity remain restless until finding their home with God, but God too is restless for salvation. The suffering and wounded God is restless while creation quakes outside the healing embrace of God. Combining the picture of cross and resurrection with the parable of the prodigal son, Park says that, "until the last lost person comes home, God's mind and body are nailed to the cross."[51] Suffering with the world and at its hands, God has refused to be God without us. "What saves us does not flow from the penalty that Jesus suffered, the

---

48. I have not been able to find a place in which Park addresses the connection between the essence and existence of God given the radical openness of God to history in his system. It seems that should salvation indeed be reciprocal, because of the very nature of love, the question of God's essence easily shifts to God's existence. The question "Who is God?" can quickly become "Is God?" under these terms. Park argues that it is the goodness of God that motivates God's exposure to the world, but this exposure to *Han* is not an end unto itself, but an economic and necessary component to the work of salvation. Should the promise of the resurrection not come to pass, would not the essence of God as described be revealed to be false—would not history testify to the failure or death of God? God's sovereignty, should God too be in need of salvation, would require eschatological consumption. Without it the very history of the *Han*-ridden people testifies to absence of God.

49. Park, *The Wounded Heart of God*, 102.

50. Park, *Triune Atonement*, 92.

51. Ibid., 90.

victory he won, or the ransom he paid for us, but from the ardent care of God," and it is here when the consequences of what Jesus said, did, and endured are understood in the life of God, that Park's account of the atonement becomes Trinitarian.[52]

The notion of triune atonement can be rounded off here. Three assertions are at the core of Park's argument. First, the continuity of the Holy Spirit throughout Creation gains a particularity and comes to participate in a larger triune mission more specifically post-Easter. Second, his relational theory of atonement that was initiated in Jesus must be carried on through the Paraclete in order for the triune God to assume all and redeem all. Third, the present work of the Paraclete is not an isolated work, but a shared work of all three persons. Park distinguishes the Holy Spirit and the Paraclete by emphasizing that the Paraclete is both distinctively shaped by Jesus and understood as a person.[53] Conceptually the difference is not one of distance, but simply that the Spirit who was always present and part of the coming of Jesus has been uniquely shaped by and sent out on mission post-Easter. Having grieved and suffered with Jesus to the cross, the Holy Spirit is named the Paraclete. Like Jesus, the Paraclete is a divine practitioner of solidarity in the presence of all crosses and a committed agent of liberation and healing in the face of sin and death. The emphasis Park puts on the Holy Spirit's renaming post-Easter is a Johannine recognition that the Christ event was an event in the life of God.[54] The sending of the Paraclete comes at a particular place in the narrative, after God's own experience through the cross—after God's own *Han* has erupted in history. While the Spirit was not absent prior to the Paraclete's sending, the experience of the cross within the divine life sends the body of Christ, empowered by the Paraclete, out with a new mission. The mission of God is one that all three persons participate in—as the Father sent the Son, so the Son sent the Paraclete to empower people.[55] The Triune mission is the mission of the *Han*-ridden one for "God bears a deep wound and seeks salvation," not simply of forgiveness for sinners, but also of healing and reconciliation for the sinned against, including Godself.[56] A Triune atonement is one in which salvation is for both God and the world together, a

---

52. Ibid., 89.
53. Ibid., 62.
54. Ibid., 61.
55. Ibid., 64-65.
56. Park, "The God Who Needs Our Salvation," 92.

reconciliation of the wounds in history and within the life of God, and a hope for both sinners and the sinned-against.

Identification and Solidarity in the Process of Salvation

One's understanding of the work of God in Christ is far reaching. It touches theological anthropology and one's account of sin, along with the nature and promise of Christian hope. And important to the conclusion of this chapter, is how these Christological themes connect more broadly to the doctrine of God. Hoping to make some connections and conclusions toward an open and relational Christology that intends to develop a richer account from having engaged other contemporary constructive proposals, the observations here will not be primarily attending to the specific ways in which Ottati and Park differ in some of their foundational commitments, such as the nature of revelation. Nor will this conclusion attempt to settle larger questions connected to other doctrines. Assuming a broad open and relational account of the doctrine of God, I will look at a few points of contacts for generative connections in constructive theology and develop how the larger concept of God's divine self-investment can be extended through these reflections on the work of God in Christ.

In distinct ways, both Ottati and Park insist that any account of the work of God in Christ should not create a contradiction of character within the heart of God. Together they reject any notions of atonement in which God was compelled by or necessitated the unjust suffering of Jesus for the work of salvation to be achieved. At no point in the ministry of Jesus, including his journey to the cross, was the Father at odds with the well-being of the Son, but rather throughout the entirety of Jesus' life we see a reflection of the character, values, and desires of God. The emphasis for Ottati is how the gospels themselves reveal a piety unique to Jesus that is then shared and taught by his disciples. In the life of Jesus, which was full of heartfelt compassion, we see the compassion of God. The compassion expressed in the storied life of Jesus is one which, we confess in faith, rests in the heart of God. For Ottati, it is then theologically irresponsible to think the one who practiced and invited us into a love of enemy would ever be the revelation of a God who refused to do so. If Jesus was moved to compassion, refused to resist evil done to him in hopes of reconciliation, and taught his disciples to pray for their enemies, the work of God in Christ cannot and should not be such that God is acting against Jesus or preparing to act against God's own enemies.

For Park, the rejection of satisfaction theories of atonement, or any other theory in which God is the demanding or acting agent in the death of Jesus, is also connected to the life and ministry of Jesus, but especially as nested primarily in Jesus' deep solidarity with the *Han*-ridden people. Yet the depth of this solidarity extends beyond the broken body of Jesus and into the life of God, for the cross becomes God's own exposure and experience of *Han* throughout Creation. The relational network in which Park envisions God's own investment towards healing and reconciliation is beyond that of humanity as it extends to all Creation, for nature and animals are also burdened by *Han*, as well as the Trinity itself.[57] The point of emphasis for both is deeply relational. For both, the experience of Jesus before God and with his disciples makes his invitation to disciples, which is an invitation to practice the Jesuanic piety in community, an invitation into a way of being. This way of being is one in which we both participate in God's good work in the world and anticipate a fuller expression of salvation that comes from God. Atonement is not just a single event, but an ongoing practice of ever-deeper living in the way of God opened up by Jesus.

Park's relational vision extends not just to the community of disciples, but also into the life of God. The Triune account is the shape Park develops, but for an open and relational theology, an affirmation of the Trinity (or this version of it) is not necessary for salvation to be mutually invested reality. For example, Marjorie Suchocki describes a non-Trinitarian account that locates this process within the di-polar relationship of God and the World, and Clayton and Knapp offer an alternative open and relational account of the Trinity that makes a similar affirmation of God's vulnerability to the movement of history and commitment to its healing.[58] Regardless of the particular way one accounts for this opening of God's own life to the experience of history, what we can conclude here is that the experience of the cross is revelatory of God's normative participation in the suffering of history. More than that, in an open and

---

57. Park, *Triune Atonement*, 98-101.
58. Joseph A. Bracken and Marjorie Hewitt Suchocki, eds., *Trinity in Process: A Relational Theology of God* (New York: Continuum, 2005). See also Philip Clayton and Steven Knapp, *The Predicament of Belief: Science, Philosophy, Faith* (Oxford: Oxford University Press, 2013).

relational Christology the character of God as revealed in Jesus and displayed on the cross must reject a dichotomy in divine character and express it. I must note here a few observations. First, it contradicts the very character of Jesus' own ministry and teaching about the one he called *Abba*. When it comes to the work of God, the Galilean vision of humility is not something an open and relational theology should part with. Second, the work of God in Christ can be distinctive, in that its telling is colored by one's identity as a disciple, but it cannot be dismissive of any other experience of unjust suffering or abandonment. For the disciple, the particularity of the story of Jesus and God's participation in it should be seen as both an affirmation of God's participation in the lives of us all and as a particular affirmation of God's presence amid unjust suffering. The event of the cross is not an abrogation of the divine life, a singular event in which God was exposed to the tragic side of history, but a revelatory event of God's identification with history. For the open and relational theologian, the word of the cross is a word about all crosses. This event makes explicit God's identity as the fellow-sufferer.[59] There is some significant variation across open and relational theologians in both the level of uniqueness to Jesus' cross for the divine life and the nature in which this particular event reveals or expands God's participation in the movement of history. But regardless, there is a shared affirmation that the God revealed in Jesus does not build crosses, but rather bears them with all who are unjustly burdened. God is not simply bound exclusively to the cross of Christ, but God is bound, as the God of love, to crosses littered across history.

One of Ottati and Park's shared theological maneuvers for creating a thematically unified account of both God and Jesus' character, in the turn toward the ministry of Jesus. Ottati rightly insists that a description of the work of God in Christ that does not look closely and include what Jesus said and did will likely misinterpret what he endured on the cross. Interpretations of the cross in which the ministry of Jesus is unnecessary are particularly problematic and have been historically influential as the church came to give more politically ambivalent and individualistic interpretations. The moment that what Jesus said, did, and endured are taken together, it is hard to understand the work of God in Christ in primarily individualistic terms for Jesus' own mission was communal

---

59. Whitehead, *Process and Reality,* 351.

in its expression of the kingdom and was enacted in community with the disciples. Noting this, Ottati gives a rich account of the piety shaped by this fuller account of Jesus. Park wants to agree with Ottati that what Jesus said, did, and endured is essential, but for him the necessary next question is "for whom?" This additional focus on the relational direction of Jesus' own ministry expands the vision, for it reveals just how the *Han*-ridden people shaped the ministry of Jesus and the life of God. The victims, the underside of history, the poor, and the bearers of shame, received preferential attention in the ministry of Jesus and must be addressed along with the violators on the cross.

One could anticipate a conflict with Ottati and Park here, but I do not think it is essential, and in fact, the two accounts can enhance each other. Ottati gives more attention to the particularity of Jesus' own piety and how for the disciples then and now it addresses our hubris. As depicted in the account of Scrooge, the cross can serve as a transferable nightmare to shock, reveal, and awaken the powerful from their prideful slumber and death-dealing blindness to the consequences of their living. The transferable nightmare is for the violators and cross-builders in history. It is a genuine nightmare because it reveals genuine suffering and oppression that the one who is awakened is responsible for. The nightmare is an opportunity for grace, not simply because one can seek forgiveness from God, but more so because one can turn to a new way of being by living in relationship with the community of Creation. The grace present in the nightmare is not primarily about one's relationship to God, but also to one's neighbor. Grace, for Ottati, happens as one lives with a new openness, intentionality, and responsibility to both neighbors and enemies.

Park's attention is also relational, but begins not with violator, but the victim. While not denying the role that hubris plays in the human predicament, Park turns to *Han* to separate the experience of salvation for one who is the sinner and violator from that of the sinned against. In one sense, Park is responding to the feminist and liberationist critiques of Western accounts of sin by differentiating sin from *Han*, rather than expanding the definition of sin.[60] Doing so allows for Ottati's more sensitive and relationally aware appropriation of the heart's problem with hubris to be included alongside an account of *Han*. The misdiagnosis in the Western account of sin was not simply making it all

60. Park, *The Wounded Heart of God,* 69-79.

about hubris, but also making all the relational impediments to salvation primarily sin-centered. *Han* provides a category for a parallel account of salvation that mutually enhances the one Ottati develops around sin. If the cross gives the sinner a transferable nightmare, it gives the *Han*-ridden people different dreams—ones in which they discover divine solidarity, fidelity, and promise.

Should the work of God in Christ include good news for all victims, a news that addresses them as specifically and personally as the nightmare of Scrooge met him, there must be a different type of dream. For Park, "God's grace is not impartial. God is more concerned about the victim than the victimizer."[61] This insistence begs an expansion of Ottati's account. Just as sin is more than personal, but social, so too is it more than guilt, but also shame. When the church does not expand the definition of sin to include the problem in its entirety, we end up trying to fit victims into a role and narrative of healing that is fit for the violator. For the victims do not need another nightmare, they need a dream of peace, justice, and healing.[62] When developed along Christological lines, the nature of this hope-filled dream can be given some specificity for the open and relational theologian.

Divine fidelity, when shaped by Christological reflection, becomes for Open and Relational theology the central concept for giving an account of God's work in Christ. This fidelity is not something new in the ongoing history of the world, but it receives some specificity through Christ that, at least for Christians, can inspire and evoke faith. A few elements of fidelity need to be delineated. First, picking up the discussion of Jesus' own fidelity to the one he called *Abba* as developed in the previous chapter, we recognize that God's fidelity to both victim and violator alike was not a unilateral act, but also required faithful living from Jesus. In both the life of Jesus and the history of Israel, there is an ongoing story of divine fidelity that is both sustained by God's faithfulness and enacted

---

61. Park, *From Hurt to Healing*, 103.

62. It is important to note that this type of dreaming is neither escapist nor sentimental. Take Martin Luther King, Jr.'s famous speech "I Have a Dream". The speech itself was an act that both promised divine solidarity with the people and the struggle and insisted on divine fidelity to see it through. The hope was in God, but it was not a hope apart from our call to responsibility. It was a dream of reconciliation, but not a false unity that denied the truth of segregation and racism. It was a dream that called for fidelity from both the oppressed and the oppressors, but the call came to the each in their situation.

through the asymmetrical yet reciprocal response of peoples and persons.[63] Second, when what Jesus endured on the cross is understood within the story of what he said and did, God's presence and activity in the kin-dom movement is thematically determinative, for the kin-dom of God is both for and made up of both sinners and the sinned-against.[64] This means that God's response to the human predicament is not accomplished on the cross alone, or even through the resurrection, but also throughout the entire process which includes the community of the kin-dom before and after the cross. Last, when God's fidelity is expressed through both the ongoing movement of history and in community, the fidelity of God is not bound to a few, a time, or a transaction. The ever-faithful God is a God who will be faithful to all of history and the full community of Creation. Recognizing this ends up shaping what both solidarity and promise look like.

Conclusion

Over this chapter, I have examined two different but powerful Christologies that focus primarily on the work of God in Christ. The goal has been to demonstrate some more powerful trajectories in their thought and look to see just how they might reorient an Open and Relational theology. While Ottati provides a distinctively Reformed account of the cross, his Christology of heart has made some substantial contributions to the ongoing reflection within the existential register of Christology. Park's attentiveness to the experience of the *Han*-ridden people and its connection to the heart of God has demonstrated one way in which an open and relational Christology can not only make metaphysical claims about God, namely here the Triune suffering of God and God's need of salvation, but also how the Christological conclusions may be reappropriated for metaphysics. I will return to this in the conclusion.

---

63. Thomas Jay Oord, *The Uncontrolling Love of God: An Open and Relational Account of Providence* (Downers Grove, IL: InterVarsity Academic, 2015), 201.

64. The author of Luke—Acts makes an important extension when, at the beginning of Acts, he states that the Gospel was an account of what Jesus began to do and to teach and that this same Spirit-inspired movement was to continue in the life of the church. What Jesus said, did, and endured was not to be his mission alone, but was to be the mission of the church in whom the Spirit dwelt. This mission was a communal one. It was the mission of Jesus and his disciples whom we empowered a sent out twice in Luke. It was the mission of the church empowered by resurrection and sent after Pentecost. It was also the mission of the Spirit of God throughout all Creation and, for theologians like Park, a mission of the Triune God.

An open and relational Christology can bring five major gains out of this constructive comparison. First, any viable account of the work of Christ must be thematically inclusive of what Jesus said, did, and endured. Neither the ministry, cross, or resurrection can be understood in isolation from the others. More than that, God's presence in the person of Jesus cannot be understood apart from his own personal presence with the outcast and the marginalized. Second, I have emphasized how the prophetic character of Jesus' ministry and his radical solidarity with the downtrodden requires the reintroduction of social and structural horizons for understanding the cross. Said another way, the passion of Jesus was the kin-dom of God and this passion must create the conditions for understanding the cross rather than be relegated to the sideline. The above discussion of the cross as a transferable nightmare for the oppressor and the dream of solidarity and hope for the oppressed provides one way of wrestling with this predicament. The key affirmation is that the good news must be good news for the downtrodden or it is not Jesus' gospel at all. For an open and relational theologian, there is often a hesitation to transfer the historical preferential option for the poor in Jesus to the metaphysical relationship of God to all people. The hesitation is important and must be dealt with directly later, but Park's account demonstrates one way for an open and relational theologian to give the preferential option a place within a non-partisan account of the divine economy.

The third feature of an open and relational understanding of Christology is the role of cooperation and participation. Throughout the ministry of Jesus, we encounter a dynamic relationship between Jesus, the Spirit, his disciples, and those whom they encountered. Often theologians end up removing the cooperative aspects when using theological language to describe salvation, but as both Park and Ottati noted, this elimination of the horizontal relationships leads to an unhelpful individualistic model. What Park insisted upon was the recognition that just as an individualistic account of redemption leads to an overly spiritualized depiction, the collapsing of the vertical dimension into works of justice is likewise problematic. There is no kin-dom without God, there is no *Abba* without an eschatological hope for the downtrodden, and there is no church without the kin-dom at its center. This brings us to the fourth feature of an open and relational account of salvation that needs to be lifted up—namely that what the person of Jesus said, did, endured, and continues to say, do, endure, and transform through the spirit, is a work of God. As a disciple, the confession of Jesus as the Christ is not simply an act of identification, but one of recognition. In Christ, one comes to know themselves as known and loved by God, to see their life together as sustained and empowered by God, and seek to discover and share the mind of Christ in which their will comes to cohere with God's will. The shape, openness, and direction of one's own love and desire are determinative for the process of salvation. This means the traditional partition between justification and sanctification is problematic.

Last, the connection between the doctrines of Creation and salvation in both Park and Ottati should remain instructive. In the same way that the ministry of Jesus sets the context for understanding the cross, Creation sets the context for salvation. This has two primary purposes discussed in both Park and Ottati's work. First, it insists that the God encountered in Christ is the one good God of all Creation. While Jesus Christ mediates the existential encounter with God, the God one meets is not a tribal deity. Second, the human predicament of sin and *Han* is not ours alone but should be extended to all Creation. Thus, the horizon of salvation, redemption, and God's coming transformation is inclusive of all Creation. This directive draws a deeper connection between the existential and metaphysical registers of Christology and demonstrates that Christology is a doctrine which should also seek to address the ecological crisis.[65]

---

65. Elizabeth Johnson has done just this in her powerful text *Ask the Beasts: Darwin and the God of Love* (London: Bloomsbury, 2015).

6

JESUS CHRIST AND THE DIVINE SELF-INVESTMENT OF GOD

The goal has been to demonstrate both the possibility and need for a more robust constructive Christology. Throughout this project, I have stretched toward Open and Relational theologians whose Christologies had an explicit metaphysical register and a diverse group of liberal theologians whose Christologies exhibited a more existential register. Having begun with a commitment to a broadly Open and Relational vision of God, it is my intention to return to the themes of each chapter and allow the constructive Christological proposal to thematize the metaphysical picture. Over the course of the conclusion, I will outline a Christologically-shaped image of God's divine self-investment. When an Open and Relational account of the God - World relationship is thematized Christologically, the model of Jesus' own fusion with the divine can be both a model to us and a means to participate in this structure of experience and a promise before us: the God revealed in Christ intends to give Godself to the world.

To frame my own constructive proposal here, I must return to the challenge posed at the beginning: the need for a three-pronged constructive Christology. An adequate Open and Relational Christology needs to include the historical Jesus, the existential register of faith, and the metaphysical referent to God. Recognizing the need for such a proposal does not overcome the predicament that such a task inherits today. The methodological opening that set the stage for the following chapters containing various comparisons also doubled as the Christologically-tinged existential starting point of the Christology itself. By unpacking how Christology is uniquely a disciple's discipline, the plausibility of an Open and Relational theology of divine self- investment now becomes possible.

"You are the Christ, Son of the Living God"

The confession of Peter in the synoptic Gospels sets the stage for this book. In light of historical Jesus research, it is a common practice to begin Christology from below. For an Open and Relational theologian, the problem with starting from below is significant. Too often, the unacknowledged metaphysical commitments entailed in the practice of historical studies are internalized. This can leave one with the history of a world in which God is not present, or as more conservative theologians tend toward, a history that should be able to demonstrate objectively the identity of Jesus as the Christ. Both trajectories are problematic because one's confession of faith is not a debate to be settled. The gap between what "they" say of Jesus and Peter's response to Jesus himself is not a gap to be conquered, but a condition for the confession itself. Jesus' response to Peter's confession is instructive when he says, "Blessed are you, Simon, son of Jonah! For flesh and blood has not revealed this to you, but my Father in heaven."[1]

Several important observations can be gathered from this archetypal encounter. First, Peter's identification of Jesus as the Christ was said to be a revelation of God and not a determination of history. This means that neither the historical experience of the disciples, the historian's reconstruction, nor apologists who proof-text from the Hebrew scriptures can compel the existential confession of faith. Second, the confession in this narrative is itself three-pronged. Peter is here responding to God as mediated by Jesus. I must note it that the confession is Peter's alone and not that of the other disciples. The confession is about Jesus of Nazareth, but only regarding the one Jesus calls *Abba*. It is hard to imagine a Christological answer to the question, "who do you say I am" in which not all three elements are present.

Third, the content of the confession itself is not yet known. Yes, Jesus may be the Christ, but what it means for him to be so is not yet clear. In fact, Jesus' later rebuke of Peter and his suggestion to avoid the violent confrontation with the powers that ruled in Jerusalem only highlights that the correct identification, "you are the Christ, son of the living God," does not entail that the disciple necessarily understands the content of the confession itself. Peter is not the only disciple to struggle here. For example, James and John both plead with Jesus to

---

1. Matthew 16:17 (NRSV).

be at his right and left hands when he enters his kingdom, still under the assumption that Jesus would become king with a throne and not of the cross.[2] In the Gospel narratives, we also see that the contested nature of Jesus' identity is not only limited to the disciples. Even Jesus himself faced three temptations, each of which can be seen as a possible way of being the Christ, the Messiah.[3] Important here is not simply the ambiguity of the confessional content, though it should not be ignored, but also the recognition that the confession itself finds its content as one lives life with and in the way of Jesus. Part of the existential shape of Christology is that it takes place as one is engaged in their faith. A three-pronged Christology begins neither from below nor above, but from within. This does not mean that the practice ensures understanding, but apart from the enactment itself, the situations that shaped and reshaped the disciples' understanding will be missed.[4]

For an Open and Relational theologian today, we can expand these three observations for the constructive task. Recognizing that the content of the confession was a work in progress for the disciples themselves can free us up to seize and celebrate our location as disciples of Christ today, while expecting and even anticipating an ongoing process of growing in understanding. The Christological confession is the beginning of Christology and not its conclusion. This means that every constructive Christological proposal can come both from genuine faith and anticipate that continued faithfulness will lead to its deconstruction. For a constructive postmodern Christology, deconstruction is the recognition that constructive Christology is just that, a construction; and it is always the call toward a more beautiful, true, and just Christological form. If Peter's last encounter with Christ in the book of Acts can serve as a model for us, this process can lead to dreams in which the very demands of scripture and words of the historical Jesus are overturned by a familiar voice in a dream

---

2. Matthew 20:20-28 (NRSV).

3. E. Frank Tupper, *A Scandalous Providence: The Jesus Story of the Compassion of God* (Macon, GA: Mercer University Press, 1995).

4. It is also interesting that when the disciples of John come to Jesus and ask if he is the one or if they should look for another, Jesus' response is to point toward what is taking place in the community of the kin-dom he is leading. These very same actions are what Jesus empowers and sends his disciples out to do in the synoptic narratives. It is as if the context for understanding and the best testimony of its veracity is a community of practicing disciples.

saying, "Get up, Peter; kill and eat… What God has made clean, you must not call profane."[5]

Before turning to the three interpretive centers examined in the future, it is important here to emphasize that the openness the synoptic narratives give to the content of "messiah" is not simply a literary construct, nor is it even an ambiguity yet to be clarified from the history of Israel. We can see it within the Hebrew scriptures that there is neither a clarity of who the Messiah was to be or even that there would be just one. The identity of Israel's Messiah emerged in the process of God's ongoing relationship with the people of Israel. It is shaped by their history of fidelity, idolatry, bondage, liberation, exile, and return. The Open and Relational theologian needs to take account of the genuine influence that creaturely cooperation and participation played in the history of Israel. Terence Fretheim, a Biblical scholar with Open and Relational intuitions, has emphasized that the identity of Israel's God is revealed in the history of this God with God's people and the dominant framework for this relationship as covenant.[6] Should it be genuine, the concept of covenant involves God risking and suffering with the people. The covenanting God is the God who shows up throughout history in the situations where God's people are to be found. The covenanting God is the one who is called by the tears of the oppressed, the blood of the victims, and the joy of the faithful.[7] When it comes to the concept of the Messiah, Fretheim points out that it emerges out of the Abrahamic and Davidic covenants as a personified hope.[8] The Messiah is the anticipation of the person or people who bless the world as they have been blessed, the true children of Abraham. The Messiah is the anticipation of a leader who leads the people to embody the way of God, the way of life that draws all people to their Creator. The Messiah is a hope that emerges from the story of God and Israel,

---

5. Acts 10:13-15 (NRSV). That the risen Christ can compel theological innovation such as the welcoming of the Gentiles is important. Many of the divisive issues in the church today, such as the full inclusion and empowerment of LGBTQ people in the life of the church ask for much the same response as Peter.

6. Terence Fretheim, "God," in *Eerdmans Dictionary of the Bible*, ed. David Noel Freedman, Astrid B. Beck, and Allen C. Myers, (Grand Rapids, MI: Eerdmans, 2009), 510-14.

7. Terence Fretheim, *The Suffering of God: An Old Testament Perspective*, (Philadelphia: Fortress, 1991), 107-48.

8. Terence Fretheim, "Christology and the Old Testament," in *Who Do You Say that I Am? Essays on Christology*, ed. Mark Allan Powell and David R. Bauer, (Louisville, KY: Westminster John Knox, 1999), 201-13.

evolves in its history, remains contested, and is a symbolic expression of the people's expectation that the God of the promise is not a go-it-alone God. Rather, God is the one who has chosen to invest Godself in the world with this people, and the fruit of that covenantal relationship is the emergence of the Messianic—a faithful correspondence between both God and the world as a fusion of God's will with the will of the chosen. The God of Israel is the living and life-giving God whose own pathos for the world and Israel must be the context for understanding the life of Jesus.

Contingency and Christology

Just as there was a deep contingency in God's covenantal life with Israel, there was also a contingency in the life of Jesus. This means that Jesus should not be understood as the incarnation before or at his conception. The specificities of any one human life, including Jesus, could not have been willed before the foundation of the earth. God is co-constituted through the evolving relationship with the world. The covenant with Israel is a particular trajectory of this relationship in which a people group's sustained encounter with God reveals the character and nature of God. Through this co-constituted covenantal relationship, we come to see the nature and presence of God in history, for it is in the context of the covenant that more of Godself can be expressed. A covenanting God is not a conventional image; it is a subversive paradigm.[9] As Walter Brueggemann observes, "the primal discourse of the Bible is that this God in heaven makes a move toward earth to identify a faithful covenant partner, responding to the groans of oppressed people...this move is decisive not only for earth, but for heaven; not only for the slaves embraced, but for the God who embraces. It is central that this One cannot embrace without being transformed by the ones who are embraced. There is no immunity for God here; embracing a partner is not an after-thought, but is definitional for God."[10] The covenanting God is a God of new beginnings; new beginnings that are made possible because of the fidelity and grace of God. However, the particularity of

---

9. Terence Fretheim notes in his account of the pre-history in Genesis 1-11 that Yahweh abandons the conventional approach of being the deity after a number of attempts have failed (e.g. Noah, Babel). See Fretheim, *God and the World in the Old Testament* (Nashville, TN: Abingdon, 2005), 69-89.

10. Walter Brueggemann, "Covenant as a Subversive Paradigm," *Christian Century* 97, no. 36 (November 12, 1980): 1094-1099, http://www.religion-online.org/showarticle.asp?title=1727.

covenants is established with universal horizons. God enters into covenant with Abraham and his descendants to bless them so that the entire world can be blessed through them. It is this primary covenantal story of God and Israel that models the relational pattern for God in relationship to multiple types of partners, including individual persons, nations, and Creation itself.[11] One viable Open and Relational option for Christology is to understand the person of Jesus in God's ongoing relationship with the people of Israel. For Christians then, confessing Jesus as the Messiah must emerge out of this history of God's self-investment. Thus, it will be argued that the incarnation can be understood as God's intention from the beginning of Creation, but we only establish its application to the person of Jesus in retrospect.

Only after the execution and resurrection of Jesus did, the disciples understand his life to have been a definitive revelation of the God of Israel. An Open and Relational Christology that recognizes the historical, existential, and metaphysical elements of Christology needs to follow several hermeneutical guidelines. First, in recognizing that the Gospel is not words about Jesus, but the encounter with God through Jesus, the responsive nature of Christological proclamations must be made clear. Said another way, the community of disciples comes into being through their response to God as mediated by Jesus. Second, the Open and Relational theologian cannot bracket out Jesus' own relationship with God for thinking about Christology. The identity of Jesus which energized his ministry and was shared with the disciples was constituted as one with Abba and God's coming kin-dom. The nature of the relationship between Jesus and Abba can be interpreted, theologically appropriated, or even deconstructed, but it cannot be relegated from an adequate inquiry into his person. Third, the Gospels are not straightforward historical accounts, and must be read forwards and backwards.[12] No one's identity is given at birth, including Jesus', but it is instead developed in the living and willing within life, so that until one's death one's identity remains open. For Jesus, this means that

---

11. Walter Brueggemann, *Theology of the Old Testament: Testimony, Dispute, Advocacy* (Minneapolis, MN: Fortress, 1997), 554-55.

12. Jürgen Moltmann, *The Crucified God*, 40th anniversary ed., trans. Margaret Kohl (Minneapolis, MN: Fortress, 2015), 228-29. "If we are to understand the truth about Jesus according to the witness of the New Testament, we must take two courses at the same time: we must read history both forwards and backwards and relate both readings, the ontic-historical and then noetic-eschatological, to each other and identify the results we achieve."

his identity as the Christ cannot be understood nor secured until the cross and resurrection. From there what was a life full of contingencies appears as a divinely ordained plan of God. The Open and Relational theologian should not let the power of the gospel story distort the dynamic openness that was displayed in the life of Jesus. Fourth, the gospel stories themselves are a diverse collection of theological testimonies about a single historical person. Jesus of Nazareth initiated the diversity of theological retellings of the Jesus story in the Gospels, but the stories are not simply stories of a historical person for the evangelists, but also of God. The narrative horizon of the Gospels is mainly the God encountered in Jesus, as it remains alive and present in the Christian community. With these four hermeneutical guidelines in mind, the Open and Relational theologian can affirm the contingency of the history of Israel, the life of Jesus, and the ongoing theological constructions about the God invested in the story.

"The Spirit of the Lord is Upon Me"

Turning to the life of Jesus in a covenantal context, the previous chapter on Spirit Christologies becomes a helpful place to draw out some implications for an Open and Relational Christology. In chapter three, I looked at two different Spirit Christologies as seen in the work of Joseph Bracken and Roger Haight. Over the course of the chapter, five key themes came to the fore as important for an Open and Relational Christology that both affirm the fullness of Jesus' humanity and the fullness of God's presence in Jesus. First, a Spirit Christology begins with the relationship that Jesus had with God. The concept of the Spirit comes from the Hebrew and New Testament scriptures and describes God's immanent and empowering presence in the world. Letting Jesus' life in the Spirit set the stage for theological reflection puts the content of his life at the center. A second theme is the notion of faithfulness. A Spirit Christology attends to both the faithfulness of the covenanting God, and Jesus' own faithfulness. The protective logic requiring the sinlessness of Jesus is not what determines his person but the faithfulness of Jesus to the one he called Abba. Throughout history, the Spirit of God calls forth in each moment and in Jesus the call came to its full expression.

The third theme in an Open and Relational Christology to which the role of Jesus' faithfulness leads us is human growth and development before God. An essential part of being human is one's own life story and the various transformations that mark it. Should this be true about Jesus, it leads to a rejection of his pre-existence, but not to his particularity. Bracken argued that the higher order divine subjectivity could continuously determine and cooperate with the lower order human subjectivity in such a way that it facilitates a constant bond. I resist this because it establishes the priority of the divine subjectivity prior to the birth of Jesus. If Jesus' own human subjectivity played such a relegated role, he hardly experienced a genuinely human life. In contrast to this element of Bracken's thought, I would suggest that it was through the faithfulness of Jesus to Abba that a unique and particular bond between God and humanity was established. The union of God and Jesus, Abba and Son, came to life in and through the Spirit. Thus, it can be seen that in the life of the Spirit, Jesus both grows and is transformed through his fidelity to God. Just as the fidelity of Israel created the conditions for even greater fidelity in the future, Jesus' own fidelity enables the emergence of a qualitatively new relationship with God. The nature of Jesus' own freedom in the synoptic Gospels could best be described as a freedom for God. In his life and in the invitation he gave to his disciples, we see a way of being in the world in which radical fidelity to God is understood as genuine freedom. The experience depicted in Gethsemane serves as a reminder that this freedom for God is not a given, but in Jesus' prayer that God's will be done, we see that he always exercised his freedom positively in relation and service to God.[13]

When the theme of Jesus' faithfulness and an affirmation of his growth and freedom are connected together, we can understand how Jesus could both participate in and be vulnerable to the destructive social and inter-personal forces in the world. To affirm the full humanity of Jesus, his humanity could not be excluded from the structural powers of violence that shape human societies. Jesus encounters violence, oppressive structures, communal interrelatedness, and builds communities of solidarity throughout the gospel accounts. As Park emphasized, Jesus was not human and yet alien to the world in which he lived, but he was vulnerable to it and the cross thus represents the utter negation of his humanity.

In chapter three, the ways in which both Haight and Bracken used the notion of kenosis to understand the fidelity of Jesus to God is here

---

13. Philip Clayton and Steven Knapp, *The Predicament of Belief* (Oxford: Oxford University Press, 2011), 83-90.

reemphasized. Within a Spirit Christology, the concept of kenosis is not used to describe a three-stage Christology in which the preexistent one rescinds divinity to become incarnate in Jesus, but is rather a way to describe Jesus' own subjectivity. Jesus understood himself to be known and loved by the one he called Abba, and thus trusted the call of God that he might become a faithful servant in and through his humanity. Thus, through the Spirit-filled fidelity of Jesus, God's will is born into the world in his person. The emphasis in chapter three was primarily focused on the fusion of the will of Jesus with that of God, showing forth the correspondence between God's investment in the world and the embodied self-hood of Jesus. Here I want to expand this kenotic image within a Spirit Christology by connecting it to God's covenanting faithfulness in the history of Israel. If the possibilities available to Jesus were not determined by both God and him alone but are instead the fruit of God's ongoing self-invest in the history of Israel, the role that Israel plays in shaping Jesus' identity and call must be acknowledged. The covenantal context for Jesus' life and messianic vocation has a history that represents the dynamic process made possible through God's intimate, contextual, and historical relationship with God's covenantal partners. The depth of the divine investment embodied through Jesus' kenotic fidelity to God is not then solely his alone. The covenantal history between God and Israel includes the vocational horizon of the people of God, the contested expectations of the Messianic, and the asymmetrical fidelity of God to the people. The covenant is a partnership, but it remains a living one because of God's faithful love. This means that an Open and Relational Christology could connect the kenotic pattern of Jesus' subjectivity to that of God's within Israel's covenantal context. The faithfulness of Jesus can then express not simply the fusion of this one person's will with God, but also the faith-fullness of God's covenantal commitment to Israel. Remembering that the covenant is itself a subversive paradigm in which God's particular investment in a particular people is for the blessing of all people gives the person of Jesus a universal horizon. As developed below, this fusion of wills is not only the fruit of God's ongoing relationship with the people of Israel, but also God's desire for the world from all Creation. When set in its covenantal context, this more robust account of the fullness of Jesus' life and work can be expanded out to reach the whole of Creation. For that broadening influence, we will turn to chapter four's emphasis on Logos Christologies, but first I want to look at the evidence of this intuition as shared in the early church.

"The Fruit of the Vine of David"

We generally understand the Didache as a church manual used in the catechumen process of new members dated around the early second century at the latest.[14] It primarily consists of ethical admonitions in which the convert is called to choose between the "Two Ways," the way of life and the way of death. In it, the decalogue and the teachings of Jesus similar to those in Matthew's Sermon on the Mount frame the overall teaching. In the Didache, the 'Two Ways' function as the instructional guide to inclusion within the Christian community. As one comes to belong in this community, they are to take up its behavior and be initiated and sustained by its practices. All of this is described before any direct content of belief is discussed. In fact, as Vokes points out, "doctrinal teaching is meager and 'teaching' in the Didache means ethical or liturgical teaching…there is no reference to the crucifixion or to the atonement or to the resurrection."[15] While the entire document is constructed to describe and pass on the teaching of Jesus to his disciples, the theological significance of Jesus' person is only mentioned in the description of how the Eucharist is to be administered. There it says:

> And with respect to the thanksgiving meal, you shall give thanks as follows. First, with respect to the cup: 'we give thanks, our Father, for the holy vine of David, your child, which you made known to us through Jesus your child. To you be the glory forever. As this fragment of bread was scattered upon the mountains and was gathered to become one, so may your church be gathered together from the ends of the earth into your kingdom. For the glory and power are yours through Jesus Christ forever.'[16]

---

14. Ehrman, *The Apostolic Fathers*, 406.
15. F. E. Vokes, "Life and Order in an Early Church: The Didache," *ANRW* 27.1:228.
16. Ehrman, *The Apostolic Fathers*, 421.

Here the community's Christological reflection is set in several contexts that the Open and Relational theologian should notice. First, those who come to this confession of Jesus Christ do so in a community of practice in which the teachings of Jesus are both central and normative. Said another way, the teachings that describe Jesus' own life in the Spirit are here essential for the converts' identity. Second, both David and Jesus are identified as children of the Father in such a way that David takes historical precedent and Jesus a revelatory one. Third, the Eucharist meal is not understood in light of the cross and resurrection, but as the expansion and embodiment of God's kingdom in the world. Lastly, the ongoing work of God in the community is understood to be empowered through Jesus Christ.

Seeing Jesus as the fruit of the vine of David is a powerful image that resonates with the Spirit Christology being developed here. It recognizes that God's unique presence in Jesus did not happen in a vacuum and that it was in fact impossible outside of God's covenanting relationship with Israel. Even the faithfulness of the spirit-filled Jesus himself would not have been possible without the living tradition of the people. Jesus may have been the Christ, but his coming is not a work of God alone. In the introduction, an initial sketch of an Open and Relational theology outlined three distinct powers in each moment as a way of depicting God as Spirit in the world: the inheritance of the past, the gift of possibility, and the responsibility of freedom. To better capture the nature of a Spirit Christology, I will return to each of them individually. First, the inheritance of the past gives a significant shape to what comes into being in each moment. No present work of the Spirit can escape its shaping power, and yet since the past is itself the fruit of a previous moment of the God-World relationship, the past itself is Spirit-filled. In the past, just as in each present moment, creatures respond to the Spirit. Since these dynamic responses make up our past and in turn shape what is possible in the present. Trajectories of responsiveness are the co-constituted means by which greater expression of divine possibilities are given to reality. Recognizing this, the covenantal setting for the messianic vocation of Jesus is a work of the Spirit in the life of Israel. Without the faithfulness of Abraham and Sarah, the Exodus from Egypt, the voice of the Prophets, and so on, Jesus could not have been the Christ. Jesus was born into a community that was graced with this inheritance and he is the fruit of it. As the fruit of the vine of David, Jesus embodies the promise of the tradition which is a work of both God and God's people.

The possibilities given to each moment in the life of Jesus are possibilities that are only possible because of the covenant. This recognition means that the ongoing narrative of God's self-investment in the covenant with God's people is a cumulative communication that expands what is potentially embodied. When the covenantal faithfulness of God reaches its full expression in Jesus Christ as the fruit of the vine of David, something potentially changes. At the spirit-empowered crossroads of Christ's kenotic faithfulness and Abba's covenantal faithfulness, the history of God and the World reached a new moment. God was always co-constituted through God's evolving relationship with the world, but in the history of Israel and the life of Jesus, this relationship fused in a particular way that revealed both a new possibility for the world and God's creative intent from the beginning. This new possibility that emerged in the fusing of the human and divine will through the kenotic and covenantal work of the Spirit makes the singular relationship of Jesus to God definitive for both God and a new potential possibility for the world's continued future. In the emergence of this new level of spirit-infused intimacy between God and the World, the intention and desire of God for the world has also been revealed. We hear this in the hymn of Philippians 2 when Paul charges the church to let the same mind that was in Christ Jesus be in them. In the revelation of Jesus as the Christ, we can see that the pathos of the covenanting God is not only moved by the tumult of history, but also that this God has sought to know it and share it completely. In this way, it is through God's self-investment in the world that we come to both see who God is and receive the gift of the divine life itself. The God of Israel is the good God of all Creation. Here the connection between God as Creator and Redeemer are mutually conditioned.

"Image of the Invisible God"

Above we have considered the need for a three-pronged Christology that works with the historical, existential, and metaphysical registers. The Christologically-tinged existential starting point of Christology has been shown to problematize the reduction of the doctrine to anything less than all three, and also thus contends that Christology itself is a disciple's doctrine precisely for those whose experience of God has been mediated by Jesus such that the disciple identifies him as the Christ. Working an Open and Relational account of a Spirit Christology has demonstrated at least the possibility of starting a Christology from below while developing the nuance of a more rounded proposal. When one recognizes the role of the Spirit in the world, the nature of Jesus' fidelity to God and God's empowering and participatory presence in Jesus, the work of the Spirit encountered in history at an existential register can also be revelatory of a God who is invested in the world. The expansion of this dynamic to the covenantal tradition reveals how the history of Israel contains the self- thematization of God, which is always a work of the Spirit. In the life of Jesus, this same Spirit not only expresses the fullness of humanity as one whose will is faithfully fused with the divine, but also expresses in a particular way God's fidelity to us.

Given the Open and Relational account of this Spirit Christology, several tensions arise when looking toward the tradition of Logos Christologies seen in church history. A Logos Christology is a powerful and historic way the church has insisted that it was God's intention from the act of Creation to give Godself to the world in the most intimate way. Generally, this is depicted in a three-stage Christology that began with the pre-existent Christ, who is both the eternal Son and Word of God. This is not possible, given the metaphysical commitments developed but coming out of the work in chapter four there are several constructive openings that have become possible. First, it is important to note just what is being rejected in an Open and Relational proposal. Not only are the pre-existence of Christ and the three-staged Christology, but as discussed previously, strong forms of a matter—spirit dualism must go as well. With this comes the rejection of the hypostatic union as the solution to the doubly full affirmation in the incarnation. A second constructive opening advanced in chapter four is a concept of participation in which the divine initiative of the Creator to give Godself to Creation sustains a spectrum of participation in which grace and growth are both possible. Here we see how the incarnation itself is God's means of salvation, how God's desire to give Godself to the world is realized. The last opening developed above is the possibility for a non-interventionist account of the incarnation. This requires that an Open and Relational theology describe in two-stage form what has traditionally been done in three stages. If this is viable, the major gain for constructive theology is being able to draw a connection between salvation history and universal history, which was a challenge that was first raised in chapter two.

In chapter four, I outlined how the natural theology that sustains Cobb's Logos Christology enables him to see the world as a creative work of God with its growing complexity and subjectivity across the universe because of God's ongoing engagement with it. God is then the ground of all freedom, the one who has nurtured it throughout the cosmos, but never the single or final cause. God is Creator, yet the activity of Creation is not a single act, but ongoing co-creative process. For Open and Relational theologians, God and the world are linked and the history of the cosmos is a history of their shared life together. God and the world affect one another in a reciprocal relationship. The source of order, call, and creativity throughout the process is God, for God is the one who gives the gift of possibility to each moment of Creation. The divine creative initiative makes the entire process something more than pure repetition. The emergent structures necessary for a greater complexity of life are in fact a co-creative endeavor, but the source of these emergent novel developments is God. God's ongoing self-investment in the world sustains and calls forth the continued process of the world. For this reason, Cobb uses the notion of incarnation to describe the nature of God's relationship to the world.[17] This naturalized potential for incarnation is an important part of an Open and Relational Christology, for in it the initial aim of God in each moment is understood to be a potential embodiment of God in the world in which the aim itself is in part shaped by God's experience of the world. When it comes to the person of Jesus, Cobb argues that the initial aim of God co-constituted the very self-hood of Jesus. Each moment is potentially an incarnation of God's self-investment in the world, but in Christ the distance between the source of the initial aim and the response to it is dissolved. This understanding of the incarnation of God's Logos rejects the traditional three-stage story, matter—spirit dualism, and locates the incarnation of God in Jesus within the larger creative work of the incarnating God of Creation.

A brief look at the di-polar nature of Cobb's Logos Christology will help build a bridge toward the Spirit Christology contoured above. Cobb understands there to be two different poles in God. One he calls the primordial nature, which

---

17. Cobb and Griffin, *Process Theology*, 74.

is that part of God that is constant and always the same. The other pole is called the consequent nature, which is the part of God that dwells in the world, sharing and experiencing the ongoing process of existence. In each moment, each pole has a function. The primordial nature of God discloses to the creatures their future possibilities, luring the creature to respond toward God's desired aim. And thus, the consequent nature of God takes up what has become history and redeems it as it is brought into the divine life. Knowing the world inside and out, God lures the world in the next moment toward the most beautiful, true, good, adventurous, and zesty possibility. For Cobb, the Logos is the primordial nature of God that gives the initial aim to each moment of becoming. God, with full knowledge of beauty, truth, and goodness—and with a taste for adventure and zest—receives the previous moment, understands it completely, and then offers initial aims for the next moment. Since mutual indwelling is natural for God and the world, the variable for bringing both God and a person together in perfect harmony is faithfulness. Nothing has to be subtracted to get God into the event, for the event is already taking place in God. The human role is to embody and give existence to the insistence of God's Word.

At the heart of this dynamic is an image of divine self-investment that puts forth the proposition that in each moment, God gives the Word to the world and then receives back into God all that the world becomes. For Cobb, this giving of Godself to the world is inherently incarnational. When we are both aware of and respond to God's call, God's will is done on earth and the Word of God, in some measure, is made flesh. The incarnation of the Logos in the person of Jesus is not simply a series of incarnational moments. What Cobb describes as the internalization of the primordial aim with the subjectivity of Jesus is a parallel description of the fusion of both wills described in the Spirit section above. However, in Cobb's version, the connection of the two extends both. An Open and Relational Logos Christology connects the universal history of the cosmos with both the person of Jesus and the disciple's salvation history. When you understand the Word of God as always calling Creation into existence, the cosmological history is also the history of God's Word in the world. The emergence of mind, complexity, community, depth of relationality, and moral responsiveness are all parts of our creaturely reality, but they are all in part the result of God's cosmic self-investment in Creation. The Word which became flesh in the person of Jesus was the same Word that was present through the

Spirit over all Creation, which includes calling the people of God throughout Israel's history into its fullest expression in each moment of becoming.

Re-staging the Incarnation in the History of God

Letting the cosmological tonality of a Logos Christology harmonize with the Spirit Christology mentioned above enables both an intensification and expansion of the kenotic and covenantal elements. The kenotic or self-emptying mind of Christ which characterized his Spirit-filled living is here understood not only to bring about a fusion of wills, but a *sarx*-ing of the Logos. Returning to the prologue of John, one notices that the Word of God became flesh—which is translated from *sarx* in the Greek language. Among the different words available to the Johannine author to denote Jesus' materiality, he picked the most inclusive. *Sarx* is not simply a word for the human body but is actually a word for all material Creation. This leads one to recognize that what was being assumed in Christ was actually the entire story of life that included all living things. Thus, the fusion of the will of Jesus with that of God has ramifications for all of Creation. For the God of the covenant, it was through God's radical fidelity to the people of Israel that the sacred canopy, community, and context for the perfect reciprocal radical fidelity of Jesus emerged. When set in the cosmological tonality of the Logos, in the person of Jesus we can see both the fruit of the vine of David and the image of the invisible God. Moment to moment, God is invested always in the world and engaged in the incarnational activity of giving the Logos to the world. In the person of Jesus, the Logos of God takes up *sarx* as an imaging of the invisible God in the temporal world. The incarnation of God's Word in Jesus is not accomplished through divine intervention, but rather through divine fidelity, patience, and loving investment in the world.

The narrative of God's self-investment in Jesus Christ remains one of salvation history, for it is the story in which God's divine loving initiative is revealed. The revelation of God through the *sarx*-ing of the Logos is this: that God has always intended to give Godself to the world that God might give the world a share in the divine life. Given the cosmological framework of an Open and Relational Logos Christology, this story of salvation is set within the universe as a whole. When the Spirit and Logos reflections are connected within an Open and Relational perspective, certain elements of divine self-investment become clear. First, there is a plausible continuity between both salvation history and universal history. If the Spirit Christology's horizon was primarily Jesus' own relationship to God through the Spirit in the context of God's covenantal relationship with Israel, and the Logos Christology's horizon was God's co-creative relationship with the world, together they represent a way of envisioning God as the good God of Creation and the faithful God of the covenant. As discussed above, the connection between these two is established in the fidelity of Jesus to the one he called Abba. In the same way that the history of Israel's self-understanding is not just a historical product but also the production of God's own continued investment in the history of God's people, so too is the cosmological process in which dynamic and conscious life emerged. The historical person of Jesus was not then an aberration within this ongoing and dynamic relationship, but rather the fruit of it.

I want to argue that Jesus is the 'fruit of the vine of David' and the 'image of the invisible,' and that these affirmations are plausible metaphysical statements derived from the existential situation of faith because God is defined as the one who gives Godself to the world. The nature of this statement, with its Christological strength and plausibility, is existentially determined because it is a constructive proposal from one who has identified Jesus as the Christ. However, it is also coherent with the Open and Relational perspective discussed in the introduction as described in much less Christomorphic terms. What I am trying to demonstrate here is what is possible from an Open and Relational perspective when its metaphysical commitments do not simply inform the inquiry into Jesus' person, but also what thematizing God's revelation in the person of Jesus does to an Open and Relational account of God. After all, an Open and Relational theologian should be open to gaining greater clarity as to the nature of God through the history of God's relationship with the world. Through this Christological proposal of the person of Jesus, I have also developed the concept of divine self-investment. It not only captures the connections between the Spirit and Logos Christologies but understands that the language itself is reflective of Christological conclusions. When one has encountered God in and through Jesus Christ, the history of God's ongoing investment in the world can be reinterpreted from this location; for the evolutionary story of emergence, the covenantal tradition of Israel, and one's own identity are all to be understood anew in the light of Christ.

"Get Behind me Satan"

The identification of Jesus as the Christ does not necessitate that one understands what it means to be the Christ. Immediately following the confession of Peter from the Gospel of Matthew discussed above, Peter pulls Jesus aside and rebukes him for turning his attention toward the confrontation with the powerful in Jerusalem that would ultimately lead to the cross. Jesus responds by saying, "Get behind me, Satan! You are a stumbling block to me; for you are setting your mind not on divine things but on human things." Then he continues by giving the disciples this admonition: "If any want to become my followers, let them deny themselves and take up their cross and follow me. For those who want to save their life will lose it, and those who lose their life for my sake will find it."[18] In this rebuke, three important themes emerge out of the larger discussion in chapter five for an Open and Relational account of salvation. There the work of God establishes Jesus Christ as model, means, and promise of God. First, one can both know that Jesus is the Christ and significantly misunderstand the content of the confession. Peter's example is powerful because he is literally telling Jesus what it means for him to be the Christ. Both then and now, disciples of Jesus continue to let our own convictions about the world shape the character of Jesus. To resist this tendency that has plagued the history of the church, both Ottati and Park offer Jesus as God's model of salvation. This means that the ministry, cross, and resurrection of Jesus cannot be understood in isolation, for the work of God in Jesus Christ must also be thematically determined by what Jesus said, did, and endured.

Second, in the aforementioned text Jesus draws a strong and specific connection between his own trajectory toward the cross and that of his disciples. Here, set within the narrative of Jesus' ministry, is the invitation of Christ to share in his way of being in the world. It is clear from this text that the losing of one's own life to save it is a participatory notion of salvation with no reference to an individual's eternal destination. If it is a statement of destination, it is one of solidarity with the kenotic mind of Christ and the people he served. The disciple faithful to the call of discipleship will, in some sense, eventually come to their own cross which entails a death of the self. Thus, the same mind that was in Christ is being offered by Jesus to his disciples. In following and taking

---

18. Matthew 16:23-25 (NRSV).

up their crosses, the disciples are also coming to participate in the structure of existence pioneered in Christ. This structure of existence has both a Jesuanic shape and centers on fidelity to God. Jesus Christ is then not merely the model, but also the means of salvation.

Third, this text depicts the promise of salvation. Here we see that a genuine encounter with the living Christ may entail a strong or even frightening rebuke, and yet in the context of the process, this judgement can serve as an occasion for grace. Knowing the narrative of Peter which follows this encounter, we can anticipate how this encounter was part of his transformation. As discussed in chapter five, Ottati's extended reflection on the cross as a transferable nightmare is helpful here. What is being addressed here is the need for the heart of the disciple to re-orient her love. By naming the implications and consequences of Peter's resistance to the cross as both coming from Satan and functioning as a stumbling block to Jesus, Peter's hidden current death-dealing commitments are both revealed and placed in a situation for transformation. The gift of the right nightmare, like a rebuke from the one you call the Christ, is also a transformative disclosure of grace.

Divine Self-Investment beyond the Cross

These three elements point toward the work of God in Jesus Christ. In chapter five, there was an extended examination of the cross of Christ as properly understood in the light of his ministry. The radical solidarity of Jesus with the downtrodden and the challenge of his kin-dom message to the powerful were essential to his identity and the Open and Relational vision of salvation developed there. The question that now remains is how Jesus' radical fidelity to God, which propelled him through his ministry and eventually to the cross, should be understood as a revelation of God's promise of salvation. The answer proposed above was that the radical solidarity of Jesus Christ was not his alone but also God's. This meant that God was not only the bringer of salvation, but also in need of it. What Park emphasizes is that if Jesus genuinely reveals the nature of God in the face of evil and God is genuinely relational, salvation is a two-way street. The cross then reveals both the tragedy and injustice of history as an eruption of *Han* in the heart of God. Salvation is then not God's external solution to the never-ending pattern of victim and violator, for God is also the victim.

The vision of divine solidarity being developed in chapter five gives more definition to the work of God in an Open and Relational vision. However, if the promise of salvation entails a healing of both God and the World's *Han*, a final challenge remains for the notion of divine self-investment—namely to outline how this Christological vision provides a groundwork for an eschatological hope within an Open and Relational theology. First, God's covenantal faithfulness is extended through the person of Jesus to all Creation. Abba is revealed to be a God who will be faithful to all—sinner and the sinned-against alike. Salvation then is not primarily for the individual but also for the community, for it is there where true reconciliation is needed. Second, the entire ministry of Jesus, including the cross, reveals that God's response to our predicament is a solidarity that runs deep into the divine life. This means not only that God too needs salvation, but that God's self-investment in Creation is such that God has refused to be God without us. In the same way that the concept of the Logos extended the Christological construction backwards in the story of Creation, the promise of the cross-dead but risen Christ pushes the picture toward a future with promise. Last, in the light of Jesus we can say that God's power for salvation is not a power wielded alone, but with the community being redeemed. This vision of divine power rejects the possibility that a potential for divine intervention could establish our eschatological hope. This power runs contrary to the nature of love and the integrity of relationships. What needs to be noted here is that our hope in God is established not in God's over-ruling power, but in God's fidelity, solidarity, and promise. It does not establish the promise on purely symmetrical relations, giving a place for critics of the open and relational camp to locate their charges, but on the asymmetrical relationship between the infinite God of love and the finite Creation. God's fidelity and solidarity with the world is not an "in between the times" relation, but is instead the very relation that gives rise to Christian hope. This hope is a promise. This promise comes from the very nature of God. The promise of the God of love is that God will be ever faithful, that the God of love is ever shaped by God's deep solidarity with the world, and that the God of love promises to bear each moment of history within God while offering greater beauty, healing, and goodness to each moment of the Creation's becoming. The process of salvation is thus sustained by the constant dreaming and becoming of both God and the world. Yes, it includes the transferable nightmares that can awaken the sinner to salvation, but it also includes a transferable dream of divine solidarity and promise—a dream that God insists is for all and that will continue to be given until all are free at last.

The work of God is revealed in the person of Jesus—precisely in what he said, did, endured, and continues to say, do, endure, and transform through the spirit. A disciple's confession of Jesus as the Christ is not simply an act of identification, but one of recognition. If one comes to know themselves as known and loved by God in Christ, and one can see her life as also sustained and empowered by God, they might seek to discover and share the mind of Christ in which their will comes to cohere with God's will. It is this life together in God for which the Spirit of God has always worked and the Word of God has always beckoned in desiring a full response. The promise and hope of salvation rests in this: that the God who chose to invest Godself in creating creaturely co-creators and who was ever faithful to the covenanted people of Israel, is the God of deep solidarity who stands in need of our shared salvation. Through the resurrection of Jesus into the life of God, his relationship with God came to shape both the disciple's experience of God and God's experience of the world. This transformation within the life of God in which the Spirit of God is shaped by Jesus Christ is now invested in the world. And now, in light of the resurrection, Divine self-investment means that Jesus is not just the fruit of the vine of David, but also the first fruits of a Creation reborn in God.

INDEX

Made in the USA
Monee, IL
16 October 2023

44701638R00102